Jay Harlow's
BEER CUISINE

A Cookbook for Beer Lovers

Photography by Geoffrey Nilsen
Foreword by Michael Jackson

An Astolat Book

HARLOW & RATNER
Emeryville, California

Food and Prop Styling: Roz Baker
Typography: Classic Typography
Production: Schuettge & Carleton

Ceramics, antiques, china, and glass:
Beaver Bros. Antiques, Cottonwood,
Crate & Barrel, Sue Fisher King,
and Virginia Breier, all of San Francisco.

Special Thanks to:
Morten Kettel, Mark Stein, Jane and James Baraz,
Judith Helfant, Cathy Michaels

Library of Congress Cataloging-in-Publication Data
Harlow, Jay, 1953–
　　[Beer cuisine]
　　Jay Harlow's beer cuisine : a cookbook for beer lovers /
photography by Geoffrey Nilsen.
　　　　p.　　cm.
　　"An Astolat book."
　　Includes bibliographical references and index.
　　ISBN 0-9627345-2-7 (pbk.) : $16.95
　　1. Cookery, International.　2. Beer.　3. Ale.　I. Title.
TX725.A1H28　1991
641.59—dc20　　　　　　　　　　　　　　　　　　　91–14928
　　　　　　　　　　　　　　　　　　　　　　　　　　CIP

Printed in Singapore
10　9　8　7　6　5　4　3　2　1

Harlow & Ratner
5749 Landregan Street
Emeryville, CA 94608

CONTENTS

Foreword by Michael Jackson
5

Introduction
7

Beer and Other Good Foods
8

Nibbles, Snacks, and Party Foods
24

Side Dishes and First Courses
46

Lunches and Simple Suppers
64

Picnics and Barbecues
86

Dinner for Company
102

Appendix: The Brewing Process
124

Index
127

ACKNOWLEDGMENTS

My thanks to the following people for their contributions to this book:

Geoff Nilsen and Roz Baker, who captured in the wonderful photographs just the blend of serious attention to and light-hearted enjoyment of beer and food I hoped to convey with the text.

Designer Dick Schuettge and typographer Stan Shoptaugh, for another fine job. It's always a pleasure to see one's words on paper, but especially when they are placed there so skillfully.

Paula Hogan, for help in developing and testing the recipes. Valmor Neto and Hubert Keller, for sharing their excellent recipes with me.

Charlie Winton, Susan Reich, and all the rest at Publishers Group West, for their enthusiastic support of this book and of Harlow & Ratner.

Beer journalists Bill Owens, Fred Eckhardt, and Jack Erikson, who shared helpful information about beer and brewing. Michael Jackson, for providing a delightful foreword in the midst of his international travels, as well as for the inspiring example of all his writings on beer. Dan and John Beltramo, in whose employment many years ago I first became acquainted with the great range of beers of the world.

Finally, a general note of thanks to the international community of brewers large and small, pub and brewpub operators, retailers, restaurateurs, and all the others who have kept alive the ancient craft of brewing and the tradition of fine beer and fine food.

And as always, to Elaine Ratner, my partner in this as in all the most important things in my life.

FOREWORD

My travels are to find the world's most interesting beers, but lunch is never far from my mind. Beer, like wine, can be a pleasure apart, but all drinks enjoy the company of good food. More than that: drink, as well as food, is part of our gastronomic heritage. All types of drink belong there. Wine is more frequently recognized in this role, but beer has been there longer . . . since the beginning of civilization.

A highly-hopped brew has such aperitif bitterness that it will demand a meal to follow. A Trappist monk once told me that the dry, golden ale made in his abbey accompanied asparagus better than any wine (he was right). A truly dry Pilsner is the beer world's answer to Chardonnay, and the perfect accompaniment to fish. An amber-red, fruity ale is the counterpart to Cabernet, and an equally happy companion to red meat. A sweet Stout or Porter harmonizes with chocolate even better than the richest Madeira.

In the town of Budweis, Bohemia, I have been served the soft, medium-dry local beer with a platter of carp prepared in three different ways. In Bavaria, there is the ritual of a light, apple-tasting wheat beer with a mid-morning snack of coddled veal sausages spiced with lemon and parsley (my suggestion that this sausage should also include capers has always caused controversy). After lunch, there has been a darker, spicier wheat beer, with a dessert of elderberry fritters. In Paris, there was a Belgian Gueuze (a beer fermented with wild yeasts) to accompany a kettle of mussels poached in the same brew. There, the dessert was tarte Tatin, with Belgian cherry beer.

In Belgium itself, there are restaurants devoted to what is termed *cuisine à la bière*. I once collaborated with the Michelin-starred Belgian chef Pierrot Fonteyne on a six-course meal. Every course was prepared with a beer of a different style. There were a further six beers, of half a dozen more styles, to accompany each course.

The London Hilton featured a week of Pierrot's cooking and asked me to plan a beer list for the event. That weekend, in plainer mode, I used Samuel Smith's Pale Ale to make my Yorkshire pudding rise, and served the same beer with the roast beef.

European countries have many native delights, but none gathers such an international selection of beers or cuisines as the United States. The most elaborate beer-meal I have ever eaten was prepared by four Belgian chefs (with six Michelin stars among them), at the Plaza Hotel in New York. The memory of that is closely challenged by the recollection of a dazzling lunch created by chef Larry Vito at the Stanford Court Hotel in San Francisco. Croutons of roasted peppers, olives and smoked halibut, served with Anchor Steam Beer . . . Arkansas ham with Anderson Valley Amber ale . . . pastry chef Jim Dodge's apple bread pudding with Imperial Stout . . .

There are many dishes that, quite simply, go better with beer. Jay Harlow has been appetizingly eclectic in his choices. I look forward to preparing braised whiskey-fennel sausages and polenta (to be served with Nut Brown Ale, perhaps?); Brazilian chicken baked in dark beer (let's be more specific: a *dunkel* lager); and rice pudding with Stout.

Nor need Jay heed the people who tease him about pretzels. This is a food with its own history and diversity. Are we talking hard pretzels (New York) or soft (Philadelphia)? I have important information concerning the South Philly Soft Pretzel. If you buy a soft pretzel in Reading Terminal market in Philadelphia, and run with it, you may, while the bread is still warm, arrive at the counter where they serve the Celebrated Pottsville Porter, from Yuengling's (founded 1829), the oldest brewery in the United States.

I shall continue to research and note such matters. I look forward to sampling Jay's future researches.

Michael Jackson

5

INTRODUCTION

I have always liked beer, but in the last decade or so I have really grown to love it. I think I was just barely of legal drinking age when I discovered that there was more to the world of beer than just Bud, Coors, and Oly. Working in the retail wine and liquor business in the mid-1970s, I enjoyed the chance to try all sorts of imported and specialty beers. I also watched hopefully as the big American brewers tested the market with maltier, tastier "super-premium" brands, only to see them fade away or evolve back toward the mainstream (the microbrewery and brewpub revolution of the 1980s was still a couple of years away).

Along the way I discovered that different beers tasted better with different foods. I had always automatically ordered beer with Mexican food, but gradually found that there was no all-purpose choice; a pale, clear-bottle Mexican lager went fine with green crab enchiladas, but a complex, spicy *mole poblano* needed something darker and richer to go with it. In all sorts of restaurants, I found myself looking at the beer list, however limited, the same way I looked at a wine list: what would be the best choice to go with this meal?

With more and more imported beers available every day, and domestic breweries producing more varieties of beer than this country has seen in decades, I feel the time is ripe for a book of recipes to accompany this abundance of great brews.

When I began mentioning to friends that I was working on a book of food to go with beer, the typical, predictable response was something like "You mean 15 varieties of pretzels?" But the conversation usually turned quickly to a great new beer they had tried, or their favorite dish in a Thai or Indian restaurant, or the beers and foods they enjoyed while traveling in Europe. Pressing a little further, I found that few of them had ever thought of serving beer at a dinner party, let alone choosing a particular beer to go with a particular dish or menu.

This book is for those friends, and for everyone else who enjoys good food and drink. It's both a collection of some of my favorite dishes to go with beer and a guide to serving beer and food together. To those who already love beer, I hope these recipes will expand your repertoire of favorite dishes to serve with it. To those who automatically think of serving wine with dinner, I encourage you to explore the possibilities of matching beer with food.

In many cases, I have referred to a particular style of beer to accompany a dish, or even a specific brand. Remember to take these recommendations as just what they are, one person's opinion. My training is as a cook, not a brewer or a professional beer taster, and I have too much respect for the skill of these true beer experts to try to pass myself off as anything more than an enthusiastic amateur. If I didn't mention your favorite beer, it doesn't mean I don't like it; there simply isn't room in this book to mention every great beer in the world. If you agree with my preference for this beer over that one, fine; if you don't, by all means trust your own taste. The same goes for the recommended pairings of beers and foods. All of the recipes in this book are good partners to beer in general, and I hope they bring pleasure to you, your family, and your guests.

Jay Harlow
Berkeley, California

7

BEER AND OTHER GOOD FOODS

Beer: A Food–Friendly Beverage
From "Liquid Bread"
       to Distinctive Local Styles
Styles of Beer
Beer and Food
Matching Beer
       and Ethnic Cuisines
Cooking with Beer
Storing and Serving Beer
Notes on Ingredients

Spaghetti alla Puttanesca
(recipe, pg. 60)

Beer: A Food-Friendly Beverage

For at least 6,000 years, people have been turning grain into beverages we would recognize as beer. In fact, an early form of beer may have been man's first agricultural product; there is some evidence that the cultivation of grain for brewing predates its cultivation for baking into bread. Whichever came first, there is no doubt that beer was one of the most important foods of the ancient Mediterranean civilizations, right up there with bread, wine, cheese, and olive oil.

In its long history, there has never been a better time than now to be a beer lover, especially in America. After several decades of brewery closings and consolidations, and a resulting narrowing of choices, there has been a full-fledged beer renaissance in the last twenty years. Classic and distinctive beers from all over the world are more widely available here now than ever before, and a whole new generation of brewers is starting up new breweries and resurrecting extinct ones, restoring some long-lost beers and ales and creating new classics. It all adds up to more and better choices for lovers of flavorful and varied brews.

First, a note about terminology: In American usage, *beer* without any other modifier means lager, the familiar pale golden, sparkling style of beer brewed by most major breweries here and in northern Europe (Budweiser, Miller, Coors, Heineken, etc.). Other styles are known as *ale* or specific ale types, such as *Stout* or *Porter*. British usage is just the opposite; what they call *beer* is a type of ale, and what is familiar to us as *beer* they call *lager*. Rather than say *beer and ale* or *beer or ale* throughout this book, which would get tedious, I will use the single word *beer* when speaking of the overall range and use specific terms for various lagers and ales.

❦

The resurgent interest in beer is a natural part of our increasing attention to everything we eat and drink. Consumers have shown that, given the choice, they will pay a little extra for tomatoes that taste like real tomatoes, breads with character, fresh herbs, distinctive cheeses, and varietal wines. So it's no wonder that we expect more flavor and variety in our beers as well.

Like wine, beer is a refreshing beverage by itself, but it is at its best when accompanied by good foods. And just as different wines lend themselves to different foods, so the enormous variety of beers and ales—from pale lagers and wheat beers to amber ales, Bocks, Porters, and Stouts—offer a range of flavor profiles that complement a broad spectrum of foods. Like matching wine and food, exploring the affinities of beer and food can be a fascinating (and delicious) lifelong study.

If anything, beer is a more food-friendly beverage than wine. Many of the foods that create problems in matching with wine, especially those with hot or sour flavors, blend very well with beer. Many of the most popular new culinary styles and ideas, especially spicy tropical cuisines and cross-cultural experiments, turn out to be better suited to beer than wine.

Beer is also a sensible choice at a time when many people are watching their alcohol intake. A typical beer is 4.5 to 5.5 percent alcohol by volume. So a 12-ounce bottle contains approximately the same amount of alcohol as an average 4- to 5-ounce glass of table wine. I know that in my own case, unless I consciously make an effort to alternate wine and water, I can easily drink half a bottle of wine (three glasses) with dinner; but I almost never drink more than two beers, and more often than not I have just one. As for calories, a bottle of beer has about 150, as compared to about 120 in a glass of wine; but since I drink less beer, I come out ahead there too. As evidence, I can truthfully say that, despite my expectations, I did not gain any weight during the process of researching and writing this book.

Beer is also a great bargain compared to wine. For about the price of a decent Sauvignon Blanc or Zinfandel in a retail store, you can buy a six-pack of one of the world's greatest beers. For what most restaurants charge for a glass of middling-quality Chardonnay, you can get a bottle of a classic imported beer or, in an increasing number of places, a pint of a fine, handcrafted local ale served on draft.

Now nobody is suggesting that beer is the only thing to drink, or that it will knock wine out of the market (heaven forbid!). For many of us, beer is simply another option, equal to wine in respect, antiquity, and appropriateness at the dinner table.

From "Liquid Bread" to Distinctive Local Styles

Briefly defined, beer is a mildly alcoholic beverage made from fermented grain, chiefly barley. One of the hardiest and most adaptable of grains, barley can grow from the tropics to the Arctic Circle. When moistened and allowed to germinate, barley grains undergo a remarkable transformation: the dry, starchy hearts of the grains convert to a water-soluble sugar (malt) that is perfectly suited to fermentation by yeast into alcohol. When the malt is dissolved in water and allowed to ferment, the result is a sort of "liquid bread" — nutritious, easily digestible, sometimes fizzy with dissolved carbon dioxide (a byproduct of the fermentation process), and altogether delicious.

Like other fermented foods, beer was a household product for most of its history. Although for a long time no one knew just how the transformation from malt to beer took place, skillful brewers learned through experience how to achieve fairly consistent results. For example, someone discovered long ago that some of the foam gathered from an active batch of beer could be reserved and added to the next batch, which would cause it to begin fermenting sooner (the first case of culturing a strain of yeast). It has also been known for centuries that adding certain herbs to beer retards spoilage. Lots of herbs have been used, but one in particular, hops, proved best at extending the life of beer, as well as adding a pleasant flavor.

Many of the classic beer styles of Europe evolved into their more or less current form during the Middle Ages, as brewing gradually changed from a cottage industry to one of larger, more centralized breweries, both secular and monastic. The monasteries, being among the most stable institutions of medieval Europe, were in an ideal position to guard and refine local brewing traditions through centuries of political upheaval. As in the case of wine, liqueurs, cheese, and many other foods, certain monasteries developed distinct beer styles which survive to this day. Long before the precise role of yeast in fermentation was understood, a combination of local water, local hops, local yeasts, and local brewing practices had given distinctive style to the beers of Pilzn, Munich, Brussels, Burton-on-Trent, and other major brewing centers. The classic European beer styles have spread around the world, and beers and ales based on northern European models are now made on every continent.

In 1516, the Bavarian *Reinheitsgebot,* or Beer Purity Law, laid out the ground rules for modern commercial brewing. The only permitted ingredients were malted barley, hops, and water. (The role of yeast was not yet fully understood, but has been incorporated into modern interpretations of the law.*) German brewers are still bound by these rules, at least in producing beers for domestic consumption, and top-quality brewers all over the world follow the same principles for European-style beers.

By the time Louis Pasteur identified the role of yeast in fermentation in the mid-19th century, helping brewing to evolve from a traditional craft to a modern science, both brewers and winemakers were already making great strides in improving the durability and shipping qualities of their products. In the last couple of centuries, as French cuisine spread around the Western world as the epitome of civilized dining, French wine (and wine in general) came to be seen as the most glamorous of beverages. For millions of northern Europeans, however, beer has always been and remains the beverage of choice, both for everyday meals and special occasions.

In 20th century America, the roles of wine and beer unfortunately came to be viewed by many people along class lines: wine was for the well-to-do and well-traveled, beer for the masses. For others the distinction applied to the occasion: beer was okay for everyday meals, but fancier meals

*Jackson, *New World Guide to Beer,* p. 43.

demanded wine. Many a person who would have preferred to drink his favorite beer with a fine meal in a restaurant or at a dinner party felt he had to drink wine because of the setting. Nonsense! Where is the sophistication in passing up a chance to drink the beverage you like with the foods you like?

Fortunately, the picture is changing and beer is being offered at many fine restaurants and dinner parties across the country. With the growing respect for beer has come a search for more flavor and variety. Over the last couple of decades an increasing number of Americans, especially younger people, looked to imported beers. Meanwhile, here and there in the U.S. entrepreneurs began reopening extinct breweries and resurrecting once-popular local beers. The 1970s saw the Campaign for Real Ale (CAMRA) in Britain, a consumer revolt against the increasing standardization and declining quality of British brews. The rescue and revival of some of the distinctive British styles of beer was a large source of inspiration to the growing numbers of home brewers in North America, already used to looking to Continental models for their beers.

Many of those home brewers took the leap into commercial brewing in the 1970s and '80s, when changes in federal and state laws made it easier to start small-scale breweries and "brewpubs" (small breweries which sell most or all of their beer on draft on the premises). Hundreds of small to medium-sized breweries and brewpubs have opened in the U.S. and Canada in the last decade; some have fallen by the wayside, while others have attracted widespread attention for the quality and diversity of their beers. As a group, they tend to produce beers that are maltier, hoppier, and just plain more interesting than the major national brands.

Since most of the new breweries are small, there is a tendency to categorize them as "microbreweries"; but some have grown into good-sized regional breweries and a few are distributed nationally. In order to avoid a smaller-is-necessarily-better snobbism, and to encourage breweries of all sizes to participate in the movement, some in the industry prefer the term "craft breweries" for brewers of high-quality, flavorful beer whatever their size.

At the same time that Americans have begun brewing a wider variety of beers, more and more imported beers are available. Retailers are finding a market for beers that would have languished on the shelves in the past. Now shoppers in major cities can choose among half a dozen Belgian ales, four or five Bavarian Doppelbocks, and several wheat beers along with lagers and Stouts from dozens of countries.

Smart restaurateurs, too, have realized that customers who drink fine imported or handcrafted domestic beers in bars and at home are not likely to settle for one or two mass-market brands listed at the bottom of the menu with the soft drinks, coffee, and milk. Many restaurants now offer a carefully chosen "beer list" of domestic and imported brands along with the wine list.

Styles of Beer

Throughout the centuries, beer has been brewed in one form or another wherever barley could be grown or obtained. But if you plotted all the breweries in the world on a map, the greatest density would constitute a broad band from Czechoslovakia through Germany, the Low Countries, and northern France to the British Isles. Just as southern Europe offers the ideal climate for the grape vine, and wine has become the dominant beverage of that region, the central and northern reaches of Europe are ideally suited for growing barley and hops, and it is within this "beer belt" that most of the classic beer styles of the world have arisen.

To make sense of the vast array of beers available, it's helpful to understand a bit about the process of brewing and how the decisions made by the brewer at every step determine the taste of the beer in the glass. (For a fuller description of the brewing process, see the Appendix [page 124].)

From the brewer's standpoint (though not necessarily the drinker's), the most important distinction is between ale and lager. Ales are fermented at relatively warm temperatures, typical of cellars and unheated buildings, and were

the dominant type of beer in the world until the invention of refrigeration. The yeast cells rise to the top during fermentation, forming a thick mat, and are thus known as "top-fermenting." The combination of temperature and top fermentation produces the fruity aroma and flavor that is typical of most ales. With a few exceptions, ales are given minimal aging, and are ready for bottling or serving on tap within a few weeks after the fermentation is complete.

Lagers are made at lower temperatures, by a separate subspecies of "bottom-fermenting" yeasts. These yeasts remain suspended in the wort (the mixture of water and malt before and during fermentation) throughout fermentation and then settle to the bottom. Lagers are also characterized by a relatively long (a few weeks to several months) and cold (39° to 54°) aging process. This aging, or "lagering," gives the beers the clean, crisp flavor and sparkling appearance that typifies what Americans think of as "beer."

Within these two basic categories are a wide range of styles. Depending on how it is made, either a lager or an ale can be lighter or darker in color, weaker or stronger, dry or sweet, mild or bitter. But this infinite variety can be organized into a few general styles, which may be named for the city or region in which the archetype arose (Pilsner, Munich lager), or a distinctive ingredient (wheat beer), or the taste profile of the final product (Stout). The following is by no means a complete catalog of beer styles, but a way of grouping some of the most food-friendly beers into manageable categories.

PILSNER   The most famous and most imitated style of lager, named after the city of Pilzn in Bohemia (Czechoslovakia). As made in northern and central Europe, Pilsner (sometimes spelled Pilsener or abbreviated "Pils") is a pale, all-malt beer with a noticeable hop aroma and bitterness and a clean, crisp dryness. Like Chardonnay among wines, this is a style that is easy to like and adaptable to many foods, from simple seafood and poultry dishes to veal dishes with fancy sauces. The original, exported as Pilsner Urquell (German for "Pilsner from the original source"), is deeper in color than most others of the type, as well as more complex in flavor.

Most of the famous northern German and Dutch lagers (Beck's, Heineken, St. Pauli Girl) fall into this category, and any German beer with the name "Pils" on the label aspires to this type. Some authorities would put all of the aforementioned beers in the next category.

INTERNATIONAL OR EXPORT LAGER   Sort of a scaled-down Pilsner style, sometimes a touch sweeter, but still more assertive than most North American "premium" beers. This is the type of imported beer most familiar to Americans and, like Pilsner, is something of an all-purpose beer. Often these are versions of well-known European lagers brewed to suit the perceived taste of the importing country. Some, like Carlsberg, Tuborg, and Löwenbräu, are brewed under contract in various countries other than the original. Others are milder "export" versions of the European originals. Beck's for export to the U.S., for example, uses corn in addition to barley malt for a lighter flavor, which is forbidden in its domestic market.

STANDARD AMERICAN LAGER   These are the familiar mass-market American "premium" beers such as Budweiser, Miller High Life, Coors, and numerous smaller regional brands. Originally modeled on the Pilsner style, most are now considerably lighter in color and flavor than in the past. They are usually made with corn or rice in addition to barley; these "adjuncts" are slightly cheaper than barley malt, but more importantly, they provide alcoholic content without adding a lot of malty flavor. The style has reached its logical extreme in "light beer," a pale lager made with even less of the stuff that makes beer taste like beer.

It may seem odd to intentionally make your product less flavorful, but standard American lager is arguably the most successful style of beer, as the brewers of the above-named brands are the first, second, and ninth largest in the world. Pale, refreshing, spotlessly clean beers, they are the perfect thing to drink on a hot day after working outdoors (in the microbrewery industry this style is known as "lawn-mower beer") or with especially spicy foods. I would put most Mexican brands sold in clear bottles into this category as well.

At the dinner table, I prefer something with more character. The category known in the trade as "super-premium" includes some fine examples, such as Henry Weinhard's Private Reserve and Heileman's Special Export, with more noticeable hop and malt flavors. One of the best of the new American beers is Samuel Adams' Boston Lager, which is a shade darker than the Pilsner type but still in the same ballpark.

AMERICAN ALE Before the microbrewery revolution of the 1980s, most North American ales were of a style that evolved in the northeastern U.S. and eastern Canada: pale golden in color, fermented warm like ales (with either ale or lager yeasts), and then aged cold like a lager. Molson's Ale from Canada is typical of the style; it is a little fruitier in flavor and has more hop character than typical domestic lagers, but otherwise is similar in strength, maltiness, and food affinities. This style is sometimes known as "cream" or "blonde" ale. A few Northeastern breweries are producing new ales in this style, but most new American ales fall into one of the following categories.

PALE ALE Mostly a strong amber in color, these ales are pale only in comparison to darker ales. The style includes the "bitter" served in British pubs as well as most of the famous export ales (Bass, Young's, Samuel Smith). This is also one of the favorite styles of newer American craft breweries, especially on the West Coast. It has produced such modern classics as Sierra Nevada Pale Ale, Red Tail Ale, and Anchor's Liberty Ale and Steam Beer. (The last is not a true ale, but it fits the flavor profile.) *India Pale Ale* dates from the British colonial days, when brewers made strong, highly hopped ales to survive the sea journey to India; today the term generally means a well-hopped ale more golden than amber.

A good Pale Ale has plenty of fruit and hops in the aroma; rich, malty, dry or slightly sweet flavors; and a hefty dose of bittering hops. It is my favorite type of beer to drink with or without food. Think of it as the beer world's equivalent of well-aged Cabernet Sauvignon: it can be delicious on its own, but shows its best with lamb, beef, duck, and other rich meats and poultry, or an assertive fish like grilled salmon.

AMBER AND DARK LAGERS This admittedly broad category covers a wide range of styles typical of southern Germany; all are darker and maltier than lagers of the Pilsner or International style. Vienna is the traditional home of a reddish-amber style of lager; the medium-roasted grain that gives this typical color is still known as Vienna malt in many other countries. But these days, the brewing style developed in Vienna is more popular among Bavarian brewers than in its homeland. Jackson* describes the "bouquet and sweet spiciness" of Vienna-style malt as an essential characteristic of Munich Oktoberfest or Märzen beers, of which Spaten and Paulaner are excellent and widely available brands. Moretti La Rossa, brewed in former Austrian territory in northeast Italy, belongs in the same category. Mexico's Dos Equis has the color of Vienna malt, though it's a bit sweeter and simpler than most. (Incidentally, despite the lack of consensus on its meaning, Amber has become a fairly common name in new American microbreweries and brewpubs for a variety of ales and lagers.)

Darker and richer than amber lagers, but still in the same general category, are the chocolate-brown Munich dark (Dunkel) lagers. Stronger still are the Bavarian Bocks, especially those labeled Doppelbock or having a name ending in *-ator* (Optimator, Salvator, etc.).

The amber and dark lagers offer plenty of opportunities at the table. In general, the darker this type of beer, the more hop character it has, although none is especially bitter. They are natural partners to various German-style sausages, especially white sausages (see page 96); but they are equally at home with most red meat dishes as well as cheese, and they go surprisingly well with spicy tropical cuisines.

The dark lagers from the major domestic breweries might be expected to fall into this category, but they are really not much different in flavor profile from their light counterparts.

*New World Guide to Beer, p. 47.

BROWN ALE Not an especially common style here, but popular in England, Brown Ales are rich, sweetish, and malty. The name is apt; they are fairly dark, though not as dark as Porters or Stouts, and they are definitely less bitter. Newcastle Brown is on the mild side, Samuel Smith's Nut Brown Ale a bit more assertive.

STOUT AND PORTER A broad category covering dark amber to almost black ales in the English and Irish tradition. A high proportion of dark-roasted malts gives chocolate- or coffee-like, sometimes slightly burnt, aromas and flavors and gives a definite brown tint to the head. It also adds body to the finished beer in the form of unfermentable sugars. Most ales in this category are well hopped; some are quite bitter. Sweetness ranges from nearly dry (Guinness Extra Stout) to quite sweet, especially in the English sweet Stouts, which can have unfermentable milk sugar (lactose) or oatmeal added to the wort. An especially strong style, Imperial or "Russian" Stout, was developed in 18th- and 19th-century England and became popular with the court of the Czars.

Porters and Stouts are among the most popular styles with new American craft breweries. In a perfect world, there would be a clear and widely observed distinction between the two styles; there is not. If any generalization is possible, Stouts tend to be a bit higher in alcohol, sweetness, and hop bitterness than Porters. Actually, the name Stout is short for Stout Porter, a label which arose in mid-18th-century England to distinguish a stronger and darker form of Porter. This distinction is really only useful when dealing with a brewery that makes both Porter and Stout. Any one brewery's Porter may be stronger than another's Stout. (To confuse things totally, Samuel Smith's Strong Stout is called Porter when shipped to the U.S.)

More than in any other category, there is no substitute for tasting various brands for yourself and coming up with your personal favorites. I will try to stick to the terms Porter, dry Stout, and sweet Stout, typified for me by Sierra Nevada Porter, Guinness Extra Stout, and Mackeson's Triple Stout.

These "black" beers can accompany a surprisingly wide range of foods. Guinness and oysters is a famous combination, and one which I urge the skeptical to try. In fact, both Porter and dry Stout are a good match with most shellfish, fish in a cream sauce, or most anything with a cheese sauce. They are also quite at home with roasted meats or poultry. I find the sweetest stouts more attractive away from the dinner table, or with a not-too-sweet dessert such as the rice pudding on page 45.

BELGIAN ALES Apart from the British Isles, Belgium is the only European country where ale is a dominant type of beer. Belgian ales offer a tremendous range of flavors, from pale but distinctive ales such as Duvel to the rich, complex amber Trappist Ales (Chimay is the most widely available example) to various top-fermented or spontaneously fermenting wheat beers (below). Several German cities, notably Düsseldorf and Cologne, also have traditional top-fermenting beers, often known as *altbier* ("old" in this case referring to the brewing method, not the age of the beer).

If pale ale is like Cabernet, then a Belgian Trappist Ale is certainly the red Burgundy of the beer world. (And although it can be one of the most expensive beers on the market, it's still a whole lot cheaper per serving than anything from the Côte d'Or.) A slight addition of beet sugar (sucrose) gives some of these beers a distinctive aroma and a softness on the palate. Even with a noticeable residual sweetness, this style is a fitting companion to fine beef, especially when prepared with a wine sauce.

WHEAT BEER Although the two German names for this type, *Weissbier* and *Weizenbier,* sound alike, the similarity is just coincidence. The former means "white beer" and is the term favored in northern Germany. The latter term, preferred in the south, simply means "wheat beer." Whatever you call them, these beers get their particular flavor and aroma from a mixture of malted wheat and barley. The pale northern style, typified by Berliner Weisse, is noticeably tart with lactic acid produced during fermentation. It is typically served with a dash of sweet raspberry or woodruff syrup, and is perhaps best as refreshment on a hot afternoon or as a before-dinner drink. Belgium has a number of distinct styles of wheat beer, including the famous Lambic, which is made with about a third unmalted wheat and two-thirds barley malt and ferments spontaneously from wild airborne yeasts. It also comes in a fruit-flavored version, Kriek or Frambozen, in which cherries or raspberries are added to the fermenting beer. In my admittedly limited experience, I have not found a perfect match of these beers with food; I prefer them before rather than with a meal.

The Bavarian style of wheat beer, made with at least half malted wheat and top-fermented, can have a striking clove aroma, but its overall balance of flavor is more like that of the ligher German all-barley lagers than the wheat beers mentioned above. Try a Bavarian Weizen as an occasional change from Pilsner or other lager types, especially with seafood dishes, where its slight tartness works especially well. Many new American breweries are producing wheat beers, especially in the summer, and most I have tasted are closer to the Bavarian than to the Berliner or Belgian styles.

OTHER STYLES   Although many breweries have used the term "dry" in their advertising over the years, "Dry Beer" has come to be identified with a Japanese style now imitated by some American brewers. A genetically altered strain of yeast produces enzymes that convert much of the dextrins (unfermentable sugars) in the malt into fermentable form. The result is indeed a dry-tasting beer, with almost no dextrins to provide sweetness, body, complexity, or lingering finish. Why American brewers of this style have decided that absence of aftertaste is an advantage is a total mystery to me. Personally, I have no use for a beer that can be forgotten a second after it is swallowed.

American malt liquor is a close cousin to Dry Beer, but the malt liquor process extracts higher alcohol levels (5½ to 7 percent by volume) from a stronger wort. The result is simply an American lager with extra alcohol (not a product the American brewing industry can be proud of). Unfortunately, because some state laws require that any brews of higher than a certain strength be labeled "malt liquor," this term is sometimes found on the labels of European classics that have nothing in common with the American product.

One extra-strong variety of beer that offers flavor as well as higher alcohol is variously known as barley wine, strong ale, or "winter warmer." These are generally dark, very rich ales, slowly fermented to an alcohol content approaching that of table wines (8 to 12 percent by volume) and often bottled in smaller bottles. Think of them as alternatives to port or dessert sherry, to be sipped as a liquid dessert or after dinner in front of the fire.

Beer and Food

One of the most basic roles of beer, at the table or apart from it, is simple refreshment—"wetting the whistle." Because beer is about 95 percent water, most of what it does is satisfy thirst. The complex of ingredients that makes up the other five percent makes all the difference in how a given beer goes with given foods.

There are many reasons why certain foods taste good with beer, and why certain combinations taste better than others. When analyzing why a particular dish or a particular combination of foods (including beverages) works, I always come back to the balancing Five Flavors identified by the Chinese thousands of years ago: sweet, sour, salty, bitter, and hot (pungent). Not every dish needs to contain every element, but when one of these flavors completely dominates a meal, or is missing altogether, the overall balance suffers.

In the five-flavor formula, beer mostly offers bitterness and sweetness; occasionally it adds acidity. Just how bitter and how sweet a given beer is determines its food affinities. When it comes to matching beer and food, grouping beers by their overall flavor makes more sense than categorizing them as lager versus ale, or by color, or along national boundaries.*

One aspect of the flavor of beer is actually tactile rather than pure taste. The bitter astringency of hops, like tannin

*David Rosengarten, "The Case for Beer," *Food & Wine,* August 1990, p. 52.

in red wines, is a perfect way to cut through the effect of fats on the palate. Without such a foil, rich foods such as beef, pork, duck, or cheese would quickly become heavy. A sip of a well-hopped ale or lager rinses away the fatty film and sets up the taste buds for more.

Texture can be as important as flavor in choosing foods to accompany your favorite beer. Let's face it, beer by itself doesn't offer much in the way of texture (apart from the thickest Stouts, which are almost chewy in their mouth-filling qualities.) A beer needs something firmer to go with it, whether it's the crunch of chips or pickles, the chewy texture of home-baked pretzels or crusty bread, or the crackle of fried shellfish or vegetables. Imagine having just a bowl of creamy soup with your beer; it doesn't quite make it. But leave some of the vegetables in large, firm pieces, or better yet add some crisp croutons or crackers, and it works.

Matching Beer and Ethnic Cuisines

Sausages and other cured meats are plentiful in the cuisines of the European beer belt, and it's not just coincidence that they go well with beer. The sausages supply salty, sometimes peppery flavors and plenty of fat. When they are served, there is usually a sour accompaniment, such as the vinegar in mustard (which also adds hot flavor), or sauerkraut. There may be some sweetness in the sausages themselves, or in a garnish such as apples or braised cabbage. A touch of bitterness from the beer completes the flavors.

Cheese is also found throughout the beer regions of Europe, and this hugely varied category of foods offers plenty of good matches with beer. Most cheeses are at least mildly salty and have plenty of butterfat richness. Some have sweet, tart, or bitter notes as well. Since one of the main functions of beer is to cut through fat and refresh the palate, a well-hopped beer is usually a good choice with cheese. Fruity or spicy aromas in a beer, as well as any sweet and malty notes on the palate, can add complexity and balance to the overall taste.

Chile-spiked tropical and East Asian cuisines are another natural match with beer. A little sweetness goes a long way to refresh the palate after a taste of something hot. Chinese and other Asian cooks understand this balance, and frequently add at least a pinch of sugar to dishes with chiles. But drinking a beer with a slight residual sweetness also does the trick nicely, and better than a drier beer.

On the other hand, a highly hopped beer can be too much in the company of other powerful flavors. Pairing a dry, bitter ale with a chile-laden Chinese Kung Pao sauce (see page 106) brings out an almost hot quality in the ale; instead of refreshing, it creates a hot-with-hot sensation. (This effect may be more tactile than taste, from the astringent qualities of the hops.) It's no accident that most of the lagers brewed in East Asia and throughout the tropics are not especially high in hop flavor. The original India Pale Ale, highly hopped for its sea journey from England to India, might be taken as evidence to the contrary; but it was meant for the British colonials and their toned-down versions of Indian food. Even the Stouts and other dark beers brewed in many tropical countries are not especially bitter.

Of course, beer goes with more than tropical and northern European cuisines. Some of my favorite foods to go with beer come from the Mediterranean world. After all, this is where brewing grain beverages began thousands of years ago. Wine may have replaced beer as the most common beverage, but the foods that characterize southern Europe, the Middle East, and North Africa retain what I like to think is an ancestral affinity for beer. Among these are olives and their oil, garlic, herbs such as thyme and oregano, tangy cheeses, citrus, spices from the East, and chiles, a late addition from the New World.

Although we don't think of them as major brewing countries, Portugal, Spain, Italy, Greece, and Yugoslavia all have substantial brewing industries. Spain, in fact, brews slightly more beer than Czechoslovakia, although the Czechs consume twice as much per capita. As an alternative to a fine Spanish sherry, a cold lager is an ideal drink to go with those delicious Spanish barroom nibbles known as *tapas*, which include olives, salty sheep's milk cheese, *tortilla española* (a thick potato omelette, sliced and served at room temperature), and all manner of shellfish. Many of the flavors that recur throughout Spanish cuisine — sweet peppers, almonds, olive oil, and above all garlic — are also good partners to beer.

Italy's breweries are mostly in the north, in former Austrian territory, but beer goes well with foods from the Alps to Sicily, and in fact it has become the most chic of drinks among the young in cities such as Milan and Rome. With the sun-drenched tomato sauces of the south, typified by the Spaghetti alla Puttanesca on page 60, I prefer a pale, refreshing lager, but the richer, more Continental foods of the northern provinces call for a range of darker, fuller-bodied beers.

Greece is also ancient wine country but, perhaps because of the hordes of northern Europeans who summer there, it has a number of breweries producing local versions of German-style lagers. In my own experience, on a hot September afternoon a half-liter bottle of Löwenbräu or Henninger was a much more tempting accompaniment to the taverna snacks called *mezes* than any wine could possibly have been.

The cuisines of the Muslim world, stretching from North Africa through the Middle East to India and Southeast Asia, differ in their particulars, but they share a love of complex blends of spices including ginger, cumin, coriander, garlic, pepper, and (sometimes, but not always) chile. Like other alcoholic beverages, beer is forbidden to Muslims, but for those of us not bound by the same strictures, these cuisines offer fertile ground for explorations of taste combinations with beer.

The immense variety of Chinese cooking cannot be reduced to any simple formulas, but bear in mind that most Chinese dishes or meals do not "need" a beverage to complete their flavors in the way that many Western cuisines do. Unless carefully matched, an assertive beer might distract from the food. An amber Munich lager or other rich, malty beer would be too much for a delicate Cantonese steamed fish or shrimp with lobster sauce; on the other hand, it's a delicious match with chicken or spareribs "red-cooked" in the Shanghai style (simmered in soy sauce with star anise and other spices).

Don't assume that when eating a foreign cuisine, a beer from that country is always the best choice. True, some Mexican beers are at their best with Mexican foods, but a dark German lager might work just as well or better. Singha beer from Thailand has always seemed a good match with Thai food, and I imagine it would also go well with other Southeast Asian cuisines. On the other hand, although I love beer with Indian and Indonesian foods, I've never tasted a memorable beer from either country. Most ethnic restaurants feel they have to offer you a beer from their home country in the name of authenticity, but in many cases you will do as well with a good international-style lager or a standard American brand.

Which brings us back to pizza. Think of all the components of a pizza: the acid-sweet tomato sauce, a dough rich with olive oil and topped with plenty of cheese, a variety of toppings which add salty, spicy, and sometimes hot flavors. All that is missing is something cold, wet, and a little bitter to refresh the palate after each bite. With a pepperoni pizza, I'll take a typical American lager every time. Leave off the hot stuff and a well-hopped pale ale works even better.

Cooking with Beer

Some, but by no means all, of the recipes in this book call for beer as an ingredient. Used properly, beer adds flavor and depth to certain cooked dishes, and acts as a carrier for other flavors.

Beers for cooking can come from any portion of the beer spectrum, pale, amber, or dark. Within each type, the best choices for cooking tend to be the milder varieties, those with more emphasis on malt than hops. A typical American lager, pale and just slightly sweet, is right for steaming clams (see page 51), although I prefer a more assertive beer such as a true Pilsner to drink along with the dish. Duck legs braised in ale (page 120) calls for an ale with good fruity flavor but not too much bitterness, such as Bass from England, though a slightly more bitter ale might be better to drink with it.

Don't, however, make the mistake of assuming that beer belongs in every dish, or that more is necessarily better. What it all boils down to (pun intended) is that cooking with beer concentrates its natural flavors. As the water and alcohol evaporate, most of the other flavors remain, so a sweet beer becomes sweeter and a tart or bitter beer becomes more so.

Bitterness is the element to watch most carefully. Perhaps it would help to think of beer as a liquid extract of a distinctively flavored herb (hops) that has a strong bitter dimension. Use it with discretion as you would use other assertive herbs.

A case in point is the risotto on page 57. Starting from a vague account of a beer-based risotto that had impressed a friend, I tried cooking rice in beer. I used my favorite everyday lager for about half of the cooking liquid. Tasting the rice for doneness, I found that the hop bitterness had become dominant. It only got worse as the rice cooled to eating temperature, and after two or three bites I couldn't eat any more. I tried the dish again using a smaller amount of the same beer, but there wasn't enough beer flavor. Then I realized I needed a beer with more malt flavor and less bitterness. I tried Dos Equis, and the dish came out fine.

This is not to say that highly hopped beers have no place in the kitchen. Guinness Extra Stout is no slouch in the bitterness department, but dark-roasted malt gives it a balancing richness that carries through cooking in a dish like Carbonnade Flamande (page 114).

Keep the sweetness of beer in mind as well. A beer that is noticeably sweet in the glass will become more so when cooked, and is probably best used in desserts (see Rice Pudding with Stout, page 45).

When beer is going to be an integral part of a finished sauce, be sure to allow enough time for the flavors to blend. Stews, soups, and other long-cooked dishes made with beer work better than quick sauces made by deglazing a skillet.

Often a more important question than how to integrate beer into a given dish is whether to use beer in it at all. There is no reason to assume that every dish that goes with beer should include beer as an ingredient. Ask yourself if a slight to pronounced malty flavor would improve the dish, and if the accompanying touch of bitterness and sweetness would work with the existing balance of flavors. If not, don't waste good beer—drink it instead.

Storing and Serving Beer

Beer is a perishable product. Unlike wine, most beer does not improve with age in the bottle (some especially strong ales and barley wines can survive for years in the bottle, and may in fact improve). What maturation the beer needs takes place in the brewery; from the time the beer leaves the brewery door, the sooner it is drunk the better. Even if stored under the best of circumstances, most beers eventually take on a stale, oxidized taste sometimes described as "cardboardy."

Aside from age, the greatest enemies of beer are light and heat. Strong or sustained exposure to light, even the relatively low wattage of fluorescent lights in the store, can cause photochemical changes inside the bottle, releasing sulfur compounds that give the beer an unmistakably "skunky" odor. Brown or green glass can reduce but not eliminate this effect. The best way to avoid it is to shop where the stock of beer turns over regularly and store your beer in a dark place or in a cardboard carton with a lid.

Ideally, beer should be kept at fairly even, cool temperatures from the brewery to the retailer's shelf. The consumer has no way to know how the beer has been handled, so here again, it's best to shop in places with quick turnover. Just because a store does a large volume, however, does not guarantee quick turnover. I have bought decidedly stale-tasting beer from a well-known chain of liquor stores in my area, and now I am suspicious of all their beer.

The ideal serving temperature for beers depends on the type of beer and, to a lesser extent, the season. In general, lighter beers are more refreshing if served on the cold side, and fuller-flavored beers express their qualities better at somewhat warmer temperatures. No beer is going to taste its best ice-cold or, worse still, in a heavy glass mug that has been stored in the freezer. (When I get beer served this way in a restaurant, I ask for an unchilled glass instead. It sometimes brings funny looks, but I enjoy my beer more.)

Standard lagers (including "light" beers) taste best at 40° to 45°. If you pull a thoroughly chilled bottle from the refrigerator and pour it into a room-temperature (68° to 72°) glass, it will reach this temperature range within a few minutes. Pilsners and other fine European lagers, light or dark, will show their flavors and aromas better a little warmer (45° to 48°); either chill them for a shorter time or pull them from the fridge 10 to 15 minutes ahead of serving time. British-style ales, including Pale, Porter, and Stout, are traditionally served at cellar temperature (around 55°), not as warm as the "warm beer" cliché would suggest. This is also the right range for Burgundian-tasting Belgian ales. Many Americans still find this a little too warm for their tastes, and will prefer to serve these ales (and domestic ales on the same models) in the 50° to 55° range. The strongest ales, such as Imperial Stouts, barley wines, and "winter warmers," should be served, like port, at cool room temperature.

Beer Glasses

A good beer deserves a good glass. Gulping beer straight from a bottle or can, you bypass your nose, depriving yourself of much of the beer's distinctive quality. (Not only that, it can be downright uncomfortable; all the dissolved gas in the beer has to find its way out of your stomach on its way back to the atmosphere.) A proper glass allows you to enjoy the beer in all its aspects—flavor, aroma, appearance, texture, even sound (the hiss and crackle of the tiny bubbles breaking on the surface).

Most of the classic beer styles of the world have a traditional glass shape. The tall, flaring Pilsner glass is one of the best known, and a good shape for most pale lagers. As with Champagne, you can watch the fine bubbles rise to the surface, getting larger as they rise. A rich Munich lager seems right in a heavier glass or a mug of heavy glass, stoneware, or metal. A tall glass with a short stem and a long tulip-shaped bowl is another favorite for northern European lagers. Belgian ales and northern German Weissbiers are usually served in large, wide goblets.

But you don't need a different type of glass for every beer you drink. Any beer will taste fine in a plain glass that is large enough to get your nose inside. Professional tasters sometimes use tulip-shaped Champagne glasses or even brandy snifters to analyze relatively small samples of beer; both designs allow some space at the top of the glass to gather and concentrate the aromas of the beer.

A good wine glass with a capacity of 8 to 16 ounces and an inward curve or chimney shape at the top of the bowl is a fine all-purpose beer glass. I also like a straight-sided, slightly flaring pint glass for ales, especially those bottle-conditioned types that have yeast sediment in the bottle. With a glass this size, I can pour the whole bottle in one smooth motion, leaving the sediment behind in the bottle. (Otherwise, the second or third pour is rather cloudy with dissolved yeast.) This is the classic glass for pints of draft ale, Porter, or Stout in pubs on both sides of the Atlantic. If you can't find it in stores, try a restaurant supply house.

Beer glasses should be as clean as possible; even a bit of soapy film will interfere with the formation of the head, and may be noticeable in aroma or flavor. Others have reported to the contrary, but I have had fine results washing beer glasses in the dishwasher. (The brand of dishwashing detergent may make the difference; I use Electrasol.) A weak solution of powdered automatic dishwasher detergent also works well for hand washing, as long as you rinse with plenty of hot water and let the glasses dry upside down on a rack.

Most beer lovers like a good head of foam on a glass of beer, with the exception of British draft ales, which are less carbonated in the first place and are generally poured right to the rim of the glass with a minimum of head. The air in the head helps release the volatile flavors and aromas in the beer, and the head actually tastes different from the rest of the beer. To many beer enthusiasts there is nothing prettier than the rings of foam ("Brussels lace") remaining on the side of the glass, leaving a record of each sip.

To get a good "two-finger" head on a glass of beer, whether from a bottle or a tap, tilt the glass while you pour the first half, letting the beer run down the side, then straighten it up to finish. Pouring the whole beer straight into the bottom of a glass will give the maximum amount of head, perhaps too much. A wet glass will not form a head as readily as a dry one. That's why some drinkers who prefer the minimum amount of head rinse their glasses with water just before pouring the beer.

When serving several beers with a meal, the usual progress is from ligher, paler beers to darker, stronger types, and from dry to sweet. But let the menu be your guide. If you want to serve oysters with Stout as an appetizer, for example, that should not prevent you from going on to lagers or Pale Ales with the following courses. Bear in mind that a full-bodied beer will make the first following sip of a lighter beer seem that much lighter. This effect is only temporary, however.

Notes on Ingredients

CHILES Many of the recipes in this book call for specific chile varieties, which are described in the notes accompanying the recipes. A few types show up repeatedly and are described here.

Small dried chiles means any of several dried red varieties, 2 to 3 inches long, which may come from Latin America or Asia. They are sold in supermarket spice racks, but they are much cheaper sold in quantities of an ounce or more in ethnic markets. Store dried chiles in tightly sealed jars in a dark cabinet; keep an eye out for tiny moths and their larvae, which feed on the flesh of the chiles.

For *small fresh chiles,* use either jalapeño or serrano chiles. The red (fully ripe) ones have a somewhat sweeter and more developed flavor, but are more or less interchangeable with the green versions. Fresh chiles will keep for a week or two in plastic bags in the vegetable compartment of your refrigerator.

OIL Unless a specific oil is called for, use a vegetable oil with a fairly neutral flavor and a high smoking point. I use mostly peanut and corn oil, but safflower is also a good choice.

PEPPER, unless otherwise specified, means freshly ground black pepper.

SALT I use kosher salt exclusively. I find it has a cleaner taste than table salt, and its coarse crystals are easier to measure in pinches. All the recipes in this book were developed with kosher salt. If using ordinary table salt, start with half as much as called for in the recipe and adjust to taste.

NIBBLES, SNACKS, AND PARTY FOOD

Anita's Nachos
Pretzels
Calamari Fritti (Fried Squid)
Ginger Cashews
Sichuan Chile Peanuts
Shrimp with Browned Garlic
Paula's Marinated Beets
Celery Root Salad
Lentil and Feta Salad
Sweet Pepper Filo Packets
Spice Route Meatballs
Lamb and Bulgur Dolmas
Cheese Board with
    Assorted Beers
Holiday Wassail Bowl
Rice Pudding with Stout

Antipasto Platter
(recipes, pgs. 34–35)

An Experimental Approach

An instant-reading thermometer is a handy way to get a feel for serving temperatures for beer. When you are sitting around sipping on your favorite beer, notice when it tastes its best and "take its temperature." For another experiment, measure the time it takes a chilled bottle to rise to the temperature ranges discussed on page 22. Do this a few times with a few different beers (not when you have company—they'll think you've gone around the bend) and you will get a sense of how your refrigerator, your tastes, and your favorite beers go together.

Anita's Nachos

Thank heaven I tasted the real thing before I encountered what passes for nachos in most bars and ballparks. The way I learned to make them (from a friend from West Texas), they are carefully constructed tidbits, with cheese and chiles applied individually to each chip. Just the thing to go with a tall cold one.

Serves 4 to 6

> *36 tortilla chips*
> *⅓ pound cheddar or Monterey Jack cheese*
> *¼ cup (approximately) diced roasted and peeled green chiles, drained*

Preheat the oven to 325°. Spread the tortilla chips in a single layer on a baking sheet. (Lining the pan with kitchen parchment makes cleanup a snap.) Cut the cheese into sticks about ¾ inch square and slice them crosswise into thin, bite-size squares. Lay a square of cheese on each chip and top it with a piece or two of chile. Bake until the cheese is melted, about 5 minutes. Let cool slightly before serving.

VARIATION For hero chile-eaters, substitute slices of pickled jalapeño chiles (*jalapeños en escabeche*) for the roasted chiles. You might want to leave some of the nachos plain for the more timid.

Pretzels

For simple and satisfying beer snacks, it's hard to beat good, thick, chewy pretzels. There is no mystery to making pretzels; it's just a matter of rolling a basic bread dough into sticks, then folding them like pretzels. In fact, the following recipe makes good breadsticks, too. Whether they come out soft or crisp is mostly a function of baking time.

Makes 1 dozen

> *1 teaspoon (½ envelope) active dry yeast*
> *1 cup warm (100°) water*
> *2 cups all-purpose flour*
> *1 teaspoon salt*
> *1 teaspoon vegetable oil*
> *1 egg, lightly beaten with 1 tablespoon milk or water*
> *Kosher or other coarse salt, for sprinkling (see Note)*

1. Sprinkle the yeast over the water in a medium bowl. Let it stand until the yeast sinks and begins to smell "yeasty," about 5 minutes. Add the

flour and salt and stir until the mixture becomes too thick to work with a spoon. Turn it out onto a lightly floured surface and knead until smooth and springy, about 8 minutes. Add flour as needed to keep the dough from sticking. Clean the bowl and oil it lightly. Return the dough to the bowl. Turn the dough once to coat it with oil, then cover the bowl and let the dough rise in a warm spot until doubled, 45 minutes to 1 hour.

2. Punch down the dough and turn it out onto a lightly floured surface. Cut it into 12 equal pieces (a scale is handy for getting the pieces of even size) and let it stand 5 minutes loosely covered with a towel for the dough to relax. For each pretzel, roll a piece of dough into a rope about 15 inches long. Cross the two ends and lift the middle section over to meet them, forming the familiar pretzel shape. Lay the pretzels at least 2 inches apart on two baking sheets lined with parchment. Let them rise until nearly doubled in bulk, about 20 minutes.

3. Preheat the oven to 450°. Brush the pretzels with the egg mixture, then sprinkle them with coarse salt. Bake until golden brown, about 16 minutes for soft pretzels, 18 minutes if you prefer a crisp crust. If baking both pans at once, change shelves and rotate the pans halfway through baking. Serve warm.

NOTE The amount of salt to use depends on both your taste and the type of salt you are using. The "rock pretzel" salt used by commercial bakers is hard, cubic crystals roughly 1/16 to 1/32 inch thick; it is not readily available to consumers. Coarse sea salt tastes much too salty to me. I prefer to use the medium-sized flaky crystals of kosher salt (see page 23) and sprinkle them rather heavily on the pretzels. With a little experimentation, you will get a feel for how much salt to use.

VARIATION Try poppy or caraway seeds in place of or in addition to the coarse salt.

A Note on Strength

There is a widespread but erroneous notion that imported beers are considerably higher in alcoholic strength than American. In fact, many imports (north German wheat beers, for example) are lower in alcohol than typical American beers, and beers derived from the Pilsner style all over the world run around the same strength. Part of the confusion comes from the fact that alcohol content can be expressed in different ways. American laws define alcoholic content of beer in terms of percent by weight, while many other countries measure alcohol by volume. As alcohol is lighter than water, this means that a typical American lager is 3.2 percent alcohol by weight, but 4 percent by volume. Most Canadian beers and pale European lagers, including the classic Pilsner style, are only slightly stronger at around 4 percent by weight and 5 percent by volume. In this country, labels provide no clue because beer labels are forbidden by law to list their alcoholic content. Measuring alcohol by volume is standard for wine and is emerging as the international standard; that is the measure used throughout this book.

Calamari Fritti
(Fried Squid)

Squid (*calamari* in Italian) is one of the cheapest seafoods available, and one of the tastiest. You can easily make an ample appetizer for four out of a dollar's worth of fresh or frozen squid. (For tips on successful deep-frying, see Beer Batter Fish & Chips, page 66). The chile-spiked mayonnaise, made with a couple of staple ingredients, is one of my favorite instant sauces.

Serves 2 as a main dish, 4 as an appetizer

> ¼ cup mayonnaise
> ½ teaspoon Chinese or Vietnamese chili paste with garlic, or to taste
> Peanut or other vegetable oil (at least 4 cups)
> 1 pound squid (preferably fresh), cleaned and cut into rings, well drained (see Note)
> 1½ cups (approximately) bread flour or all-purpose flour
> Salt
> Lemon or lime wedges

1. Combine the mayonnaise and chili paste and set aside for the flavors to blend. Before serving, taste for seasoning and adjust as necessary.

2. Pour at least 2 inches of oil into a wok or other deep pan; be sure the oil is at least 2 inches below the top of the pan to prevent boiling over. Fix a frying thermometer on the edge of the pan. Heat the oil to 400°, then turn the heat to medium-low.

3. Dredge a third to half of the squid in the flour; transfer it to a frying basket or coarse strainer and shake off the excess flour. If using a frying basket, lower it into the oil; otherwise, carefully drop the squid into the oil. Fry to a light golden brown, about 1 minute; remove with a wire skimmer. Drain for a few seconds over the oil, then transfer to a tray lined with paper towels. Wait for the oil to return to 400° before frying the remaining squid. Sprinkle the fried squid with salt and serve immediately, with a squeeze of lemon or lime and the mayonnaise sauce for dipping.

NOTE To clean squid, start by separating all the tentacles from the heads, cutting across as close as possible to the eyes. Squeeze out and discard the hard, pea-sized beak in the center of each cluster of tentacles. Give the tentacles a quick rinse and drain them in a colander.

The second step depends on how the squid will be used. To clean the mantle (the saclike "body" of the squid) for cutting into rings, grasp the

mantle in one hand and the head in the other and pull apart; the entrails will pull out attached to the head. Pull the transparent quill out of each mantle. Discard everything but the tentacles and mantles. Running a little water into each mantle to open it up, reach in with a finger and pull out any entrails remaining inside. (Working over a second colander to catch all the debris will make cleanup easier.) There is no need to remove the spotted outer skin. Transfer the cleaned mantles to a cutting board, slice them crosswise into rings about ½ inch wide, and add them to the tentacles in the colander. Give everything another rinse and drain thoroughly.

To clean the mantles Chinese style for stir-frying (see Note page 28), simply slit the mantles open lengthwise, open them up flat, and scrape away all the entrails and the quill. Pull off the spotted outer skin and cut the mantles into pieces about 2 inches square, rinse, and drain. For a decorative touch, score each piece with shallow diagonal cuts every ½ inch or so in a diamond pattern; when cooked, the pieces will curl up like tiny pine cones.

Seasoned Nuts

Beer and nuts are a time-honored combination. While you can't beat the convenience of opening a can or jar of seasoned nuts, making your own allows you more choice of "flavors." The techniques in the two recipes here can be adapted to other nuts such as blanched whole almonds or walnut or pecan halves. Walnuts and pecans especially benefit from the soaking step, which leaches out their bitter tannins.

If there is a Chinese market in your area, it's likely to be the cheapest source of bulk raw peanuts and cashews. Health food stores are another source.

Ginger Cashews

Cashews have plenty of sweet, nutty flavor of their own, so all they need is a bit of surface flavor. Dried ginger, which is both hot and slightly sweet, makes a perfect match.

Makes 1 cup

> *1 cup peanut oil*
> *1 cup raw cashews*
> *2 teaspoons powdered ginger*
> *Scant teaspoon kosher salt*

Have a heatproof container (such as a clean, dry saucepan or a large heatproof glass measuring cup) ready with a wire strainer over it. Heat a wok or small, deep skillet over medium-high heat. Add the oil and heat until a cashew sizzles instantly when added to the oil. Add the cashews all at once and cook, stirring occasionally, until the nuts are a pale golden brown, 45 seconds to 1 minute. Turn off the heat and pour the oil and nuts through the strainer. Return the nuts to the pan, sprinkle them with the ginger and salt, and stir to coat them evenly with the seasonings. Drain the nuts on a plate lined with paper towels until cool, then serve them at room temperature in a small bowl.

VARIATION Use curry powder or Garam Masala (page 69) in place of the ginger.

Sichuan Chile Peanuts

The problem with peanuts is getting flavor into the bland center of the nuts. The best way is the technique commercial packers use: steeping the nuts in seasoned water then drying them with heat to get rid of the water, leaving the seasonings behind. A final step of cooking them in seasoned oil adds more spice flavor to the surface.

These subtly hot peanuts get their flavor from dried chiles and Sichuan peppercorns, the fragrant dried berries of an Asian tree. Sichuan peppercorns are not really hot, but have a unique, slightly tongue-numbing flavor that blends well with other flavors. Look for bags of the reddish-brown berries in Asian groceries and some specialty stores.

Makes 1 cup

> 1 cup water
> 2 teaspoons salt
> 4 teaspoons Sichuan peppercorns
> 1 cup raw peanuts
> ⅓ cup peanut oil
> 4 small dried chiles, crumbled **or** 1 teaspoon red pepper flakes
> 1 slice fresh ginger, bruised

1. Bring the water, salt, and 3 teaspoons of the Sichuan peppercorns to a boil in a small saucepan. Add the peanuts and simmer 15 minutes.

2. While the nuts are simmering, warm a wok or small saucepan over medium heat. Add the oil, the remaining Sichuan peppercorns, chiles, and ginger, turn the heat to low, and cook until the chiles and ginger are both sizzling. Remove from the heat, cover, and set aside.

3. Preheat the oven to 300°. Drain the nuts and peppercorns through a fine sieve, catching both the nuts and the peppercorns. Spread them on a baking sheet and bake until they taste nearly dry but have not browned, about 10 minutes. Remove the pan from the oven, and when the nuts are cool enough to handle, pick them out and discard the peppercorns. The nuts are now ready for cooking in the seasoned oil, or you may let them sit for a few hours.

4. Return the pan of oil to medium heat. When a peanut added to the oil sizzles immediately, add all the nuts and cook, stirring constantly, until they are golden brown. Remove the nuts with a slotted spoon, or pour the contents of the pan through a heatproof strainer into a clean, dry, heatproof container. Drain the nuts on paper towels until cool; serve at room temperature. Strain and reserve the flavored oil to use in small quantities for stir-frying or dressing Asian-style noodles.

More ideas for beer nibbles:
Fried Okra (page 54).

Deep-fried oysters, scallops, or clams with your choice of coatings: rolled in corn meal as in Fried Okra (page 54), dusted with flour as in Calamari Fritti (page 28), or dipped in the beer batter for Fish & Chips (page 66).

Cornbread (page 55), especially the cheese or green chile variations.

Kielbasa, andouille, or other fully cooked smoked sausage cut into bite-size rounds and briefly warmed in a skillet or oven. Serve with toothpicks, small slices of bread, and your choice of mustard.

Shrimp with Browned Garlic

Mention Spanish *tapas,* those little savory dishes designed to go with drinks and conversation, and most people think of sherry. But in Spain tapas are served in all sorts of establishments including *cervecerías,* bars that specialize in beer and foods to accompany it—especially shellfish. This simple dish, a perfect accompaniment to a fine Pilsner, is a great way to start your exploration of shellfish tapas. Try to get a few bits of garlic, made mellow and nutty by slow browning in oil, clinging to each shrimp. I wouldn't blame you a bit if you dunk bread in the bowl when the shrimp are gone.

Serves 2 to 4

> *½ pound medium or large raw shrimp, peeled and deveined*
> *2 teaspoons kosher salt, if using frozen shrimp*
> *2 tablespoons olive oil*
> *1 large clove garlic, peeled and minced*
> *Freshly ground black pepper, to taste*
> *1 tablespoon lemon juice*
> *1 teaspoon chopped parsley*

1. If using frozen shrimp, after peeling and deveining place them in a bowl and sprinkle them with a teaspoon of kosher salt. Toss to distribute the salt evenly, let stand 1 minute (no longer), then rinse by running cold water into the bowl. Drain in a colander, then return the shrimp to the bowl and repeat the process. Drain thoroughly and pat dry. Refrigerate until ready to use. (This salt-leaching is not necessary for fresh shrimp.)

2. Combine the oil and garlic in a medium skillet over low heat. Cook until the garlic is light brown, about 3 minutes. Add the shrimp, in one layer if possible, and a generous grinding of pepper and cook until the shrimp turn opaque, 4 to 5 minutes. Transfer the shrimp to a bowl with a slotted spoon. Stir the lemon juice into the oil in the skillet, then pour the mixture over the shrimp. Sprinkle with parsley. Serve warm or at room temperature, with bread for dunking in the garlicky oil.

VARIATION An authentic Spanish version of this dish would have a small dried chile crumbled into the oil as the garlic begins to brown.

CEVICHE Marinate small cubes of white fish, sliced scallops, or small peeled shrimp in lime or lemon juice until they turn opaque and look and taste cooked. (Because the fish is never cooked, ask your fishmonger for a variety that is suitable for eating raw. Some types can carry parasites that are not killed by the pickling process.) Add minced onion and green chile, diced tomato, chopped cilantro, and salt to taste. Serve well chilled in small glasses or bowls.

Antipasto

If *antipasto* brings to mind a refrigerated plate with a couple of slices of salami and provolone and a few raw vegetables— something to nibble on until the pizza or pasta arrives—then you haven't tasted the real thing. True antipasto is a generous assortment of enticing raw, cooked, and marinated foods, frequently displayed on a table near the entrance of a restaurant in Italy.

An assortment of antipasto dishes can stand on its own as a party buffet, or be a first course in a meal. Like all good appetizers, antipasto dishes should be highly seasoned to perk up the taste buds at the beginning of a meal. Any antipasto dish can be served alone, but part of the appeal of an antipasto spread is its diversity of flavors and textures. Depending on the setting and the occasion, you may wish to compose individual plates in the kitchen or set out serving dishes on a buffet or sideboard. Serve with a good international-style lager or Pilsner.

Paula's Marinated Beets

There's nothing wrong with pickled red beets straight from the jar, except that they seem a little boring next to more colorful beet varieties. Chioggia beets, with their pink and white rings, or golden orange beets are beautiful and delicious marinated, especially when the marinade contains fresh citrus juices and your own spices. In a pinch, drain and slice plain canned (not pickled) beets and toss them in the marinade.

Makes 2 cups

> 1 pound beets (golden, Chioggia, or red)
> 1 teaspoon unseasoned rice vinegar
> 2 teaspoons orange juice
> ½ teaspoon lemon juice
> ⅛ teaspoon anise seed, crushed
> Salt, to taste
> 3 tablespoons olive oil

Preheat the oven to 425°. Wash the beets and cut off the tops. Place the beets in a shallow baking dish and pour in ½ inch of water. Cover with a lid or foil and bake until tender, 50 to 60 minutes. Allow to cool, then slip off the skins and cut the beets into 6 to 8 wedges, depending on size. Combine the vinegar, juices, anise seed, and salt in a mixing bowl, then whisk in the oil. Add the beets, toss to coat well, and let stand 1 hour at room temperature before serving.

Celery Root Salad

Celery root *rémoulade* (fine shreds in a dressing thickened with mustard) is more French than Italian, but it fits in well in an antipasto platter. Celery roots are about the size of a softball, with rough brown skin and green leafy stalks starting to shoot out the top.

Makes 2 cups

> 1 celery root, about 1 pound
> 1 tablespoon Dijon-style mustard
> 1 teaspoon lemon juice
> 2 tablespoons olive oil
> Salt and white pepper, to taste

1. Cut away all the outer skin from the celery root and trim the root and stem ends, leaving only the white heart. Slice the root thinly, then stack

up the slices and slice again, making matchstick shreds. Boil in lightly salted water until just tender, about 1 minute. Drain, rinse with cold water, and drain again.

2. Combine the mustard and lemon juice in a mixing bowl. Add the oil gradually, whisking constantly, until quite smooth and thick. Season to taste with salt and pepper. Add the celery root shreds and toss to combine. Chill until 30 minutes before serving.

Lentil and Feta Salad

The salty-sour tang of feta cheese contrasts beautifully with the bland, bean-y taste of lentils in this simple salad. Small French lentils sold in boxes are quite a bit more expensive than the ordinary kind, but they are arguably worth the price, as they keep their texture better in a salad.

Makes 2 cups

>   *1 cup lentils*
>   *1 tablespoon mild vinegar (rice or white wine)*
>   *1½ teaspoons lemon juice*
>   *½ teaspoon salt*
>   *Freshly ground pepper, to taste*
>   *3 tablespoons olive oil*
>   *½ teaspoon minced garlic*
>   *2 tablespoons finely diced celery*
>   *2 tablespoons red or yellow bell pepper*
>   *2 tablespoons chopped parsley*
>   *¼ pound feta or fresh goat cheese, crumbled*

Boil the lentils in ample unsalted water until just tender but not mushy; drain. In a small mixing bowl, combine the vinegar, lemon juice, salt, and pepper and stir until the salt dissolves. Stir in the oil and garlic, then the lentils. Let stand until thoroughly cool. Stir in the celery, bell pepper, and parsley and taste for seasoning (taste a little feta along with the lentils for the overall balance) and adjust if necessary. Serve in a shallow bowl, with the cheese crumbled over the top.

An Antipasto Platter
Paula's Marinated Beets
Celery Root Salad
Lentil and Feta Salad
Roasted and Peeled Peppers (see page 61)
Assorted Olives
Dry Salami or Coppa

Sweet Pepper Filo Packets

Greek-style savory pastries made with paper-thin filo dough are an ideal hot hors d'oeuvre for parties as well as a great first course (see Menu Note). This version combines tangy feta cheese and sweet roasted peppers, one of my favorite combinations.

Makes 24

> ¼ *cup pine nuts*
> ¼ *pound feta cheese*
> ½ *of a beaten egg*
> 1 *tablespoon chopped fresh mint*
> 1 *cup roasted and peeled sweet red or yellow peppers, diced*
> ¼ *pound unsalted butter, melted*
> 1 *pound filo dough*

1. Toast the pine nuts in a small, dry skillet over medium heat, shaking or stirring constantly so they brown evenly. Set them aside in a small bowl to cool. Combine the feta, egg, and mint in a bowl and beat until the cheese is crumbly. Place the cheese mixture, peppers, and pine nuts in separate bowls, with a spoon in each. Have the melted butter, a good-sized pastry brush, and a pair of scissors close at hand.

2. Preheat the oven to 400°. Unroll the filo and lay it out flat. Carefully peel off one sheet and lay it on a clean, dry work surface, with the shorter side toward you. Keep the rest of the filo covered with a slightly damp towel so it won't dry out. Brush the right half of the sheet with butter and fold the left half over it, making a long, thin rectangle. Cut the rectangle in half lengthwise, giving you 2 long strips.

3. Place a thin layer of red pepper about ½ inch in from the near end of one of the strips. Top it with a heaping teaspoon of the cheese mixture and a few pine nuts. Fold the end of the dough over the stuffing diagonally, forming a point. Brush the top of the dough with butter, then fold the triangle into the rest of the sheet with a series of folds as if folding a flag. Keep track of which way the filling is turned and try to finish with the nuts on top. Fold any excess dough under, making a seam on the bottom. Repeat with the remaining filo dough and filling.

4. Place the packets on an ungreased baking sheet, brush the tops with melted butter, and bake until golden brown and puffy, about 20 minutes. Let cool slightly before serving.

MENU NOTE Try a larger version of these light, crisp packets as a first course with a fine lager; follow with a meat course and a fuller-bodied beer. To make first-course packets, leave the filo rectangle whole (step 2) and use twice as much of each filling ingredient per packet. Center the filling an inch or two in from the near end of the filo. Fold the two long edges in toward the middle to cover the filling. Brush the top with melted butter, then fold the filled portion over and over, forming a neat square or rectangular package. Serve each person 2 packets on a bed of salad greens. Serves 6.

Spice Route Meatballs

Meatballs are a favorite all over the world; this version draws on lots of traditions. The lamb and the basic seasonings reflect Indian and Middle Eastern cuisines. The cooking technique (steaming) and the water chestnuts are Chinese. To top it off, they are served Cambodian style, with soft lettuce leaves for wrapping. Serve them as an appetizer with your favorite lager, or as part of an Asian-style meal with several small dishes.

Makes 18 (serves 4 to 6)

> *½ pound ground lamb, beef, or veal*
> *½ cup very finely diced water chestnuts or jicama*
> *1 teaspoon minced garlic*
> *2 teaspoons minced ginger*
> *¼ teaspoon* **garam masala** *(see page 69)*
> *1 tablespoon chopped parsley or cilantro*
> *Scant ½ teaspoon salt*
> *⅛ teaspoon pepper*
> *Tender lettuce leaves*
> *Spicy Tomato Sauce (page 40)*

1. Combine all the ingredients except the lettuce leaves and tomato sauce in a bowl and beat with a spoon or knead by hand until thoroughly blended. Cook a bit of the mixture in a skillet or in boiling water and taste for seasoning; correct if necessary. With moistened hands, roll the meat into 1-inch balls.

2. Arrange the meatballs so they do not touch on a plate that will fit inside a bamboo steamer (or directly in a finely perforated metal steamer). Bring the water in the bottom of the steamer to a rolling boil, put the steaming tray in place, cover, and cook until the meatballs are done to the center, about 8 minutes (cut a meatball open to check for doneness). If not serving immediately, turn off the heat under the steamer and remove the cover for a few seconds to let the heat dissipate, then replace the cover to keep the meatballs warm.

3. To serve, partially split each meatball and set them out on a platter with lettuce leaves on the side. Place a meatball inside a leaf, add tomato sauce to taste, and wrap up for eating out of hand.

VARIATION   If you prefer, you can cook the meatballs in a lightly oiled, covered skillet over medium heat.

Beer as Food

Beer is one of the most nutritious of alcoholic beverages. The U.S. Department of Agriculture gives the following composition and nutritional values for a 12-ounce bottle of typical American lager:
> 92 percent water
> 151 calories (approximately 100 of them from alcohol)
> 1.1 grams protein
> 0 grams fat
> 13.7 grams carbohydrate
> 25 mg sodium
> measurable quantities of calcium, potassium, phosphorus, and several B-vitamins (including an impressive 15 to 20 percent of the adult recommended daily allowance for vitamin B6 and niacin)

A maltier lager or ale would undoubtedly register higher in all the non-alcohol nutrients. This doesn't mean you should drink five beers a day to get your full dose of B-vitamins; moderation is the key with beer as with all alcoholic beverages.

Spicy Tomato Sauce

Makes ½ cup

> *½ cup finely diced tomato*
> *Dab of Vietnamese, Thai, or Indonesian prepared chili paste or Moroccan* **harissa**
> *Pinch of salt*
> *Pinch of sugar*

Combine all the ingredients. Let stand 15 minutes and taste for seasoning; adjust if necessary.

Lamb and Bulgur Dolmas

This is a lively variation on Greek-Turkish-Levantine stuffed grape leaves. For the filling, ground lamb, spiced like the Moroccan lamb sausage *merguez,* is combined with bulgur wheat, which gives an earthier taste than the usual rice. Dolmas are especially convenient for parties, as they can be cooked several days ahead of time.

Makes about 40

> ⅔ *cup bulgur wheat*
> ⅔ *pound ground lamb*
> *2 tablespoons olive oil*
> *1½ teaspoons minced garlic*
> *2 teaspoons paprika*
> *½ teaspoon ground cumin*
> *½ teaspoon ground coriander seeds*
> *¼ teaspoon ground cinnamon*
> *Pinch of cayenne pepper*
> *2 teaspoons* **each** *minced parsley and fresh coriander*
> *½ teaspoon salt*
> *Freshly ground pepper to taste*
> *40 bottled grape leaves (approximately)*
> *Juice of 1 lemon*

1. Add a pinch of salt to 1⅓ cups of water and bring it to a boil. Add the bulgur, bring the water back to a boil, cover, and cook over low heat until all the water is absorbed, about 20 minutes. Remove the cover, fluff the bulgur with a fork, replace the cover, and let cool.

2. Crumble the lamb into a skillet and cook over medium heat until it loses

Etc.

For other Mediterranean-style "little foods" to go with beer, I can recommend just about anything in the first three chapters of *The Mediterranean Kitchen* by Joyce Goldstein (Morrow, 1989). When in San Francisco, don't miss a chance to eat at her restaurant, Square One.

its raw color; remove with a slotted spoon. Pour out and reserve the drippings. Add 1 tablespoon of the oil and the garlic, spices, and herbs to the pan and cook, stirring, until quite fragrant, about 1 minute. Add the meat and cook, stirring, until the meat is well coated with the spices. Remove from the heat and combine with the bulgur. Discard the fat from the meat drippings and add them to the bulgur mixture. Season to taste with salt, and additional pepper if needed.

3. Remove the grape leaves carefully from the jar (see Note). Lay out a leaf with the dull side up and the stem end toward you; trim off the stem. Place a level tablespoon of the filling crosswise in the center. Fold the near corners of the leaf over the filling, then fold in the sides and roll into a snug cylinder about 2 inches long. Repeat with the remaining leaves and filling.

4. Preheat the oven to 350°. Pack the finished rolls close together in a 9- by 13-inch baking pan. Add ¼ inch of water. Drizzle the lemon juice and about 1 tablespoon olive oil over the top of the rolls. Cover the pan tightly with foil and bake 35 to 40 minutes. Let the rolls cool in the pan, then refrigerate. Serve cold, at room temperature, or reheated for about 15 minutes in a 350° oven.

NOTE Getting a roll of grape leaves out of its jar can be tricky, as they seem to swell after they are packed. The best way I know is to turn the jar upside down over a bowl, letting the brine dribble out as you squeeze and wiggle the roll out the neck of the jar. The reason for the bowl is to save the brine to store the unused leaves in the jar. Plan to use the rest soon; as with any pickled product, handling the leaves with your fingers leaves tiny traces of skin oils on them and shortens their shelf life.

"Good ale, the true and proper drink of Englishmen. He is not deserving of the name of Englishman who speaketh against ale, that is good ale."

—George Borrow
Beer

Cheese Board with Assorted Beers

A spread of cheeses and accompaniments makes excellent party fare, or a nice alternative to a sweet dessert after dinner. The key to a good cheese board is an assortment of cheese types, offering a variety of flavors and textures. Use the following suggestions as a guide, but don't feel you have to offer all of the cheeses or garnishes listed. The quantities here are for a party for about a dozen people; to adjust for a smaller or larger crowd, figure on a total of 3 to 4 ounces of cheese per person. Allow a little more if serving a lot of varieties (you don't want the most popular variety to disappear in the first 5 minutes). If you can't find the cheeses listed, a good cheese shop should be able to supply alternatives.

Keep the assortment of beers small; too many options make things confusing. In general, I prefer amber or dark beers with cheese; most pale lagers just don't seem to hold their own, especially with the stronger varieties of cheese. A good selection might be a Bavarian-style Oktoberfest beer, a dry, well-hopped Pale Ale or Porter, and a sweet dark beer such as English Stout or German Doppelbock.

Serves 12

2½ to 3 pounds cheese
(choose 3 to 6 of the following categories)
A soft-ripened, white-rind cheese: Brie or Camembert
A mild, semisoft, rindless cheese: Monterey Jack, Teleme, Bel Paese, or
*   Cream Havarti*
A sharp Cheddar type: English, Canadian, or domestic aged Cheddar;
*   English Cheshire; Caerphilly; or Wensleydale*
A firm Alpine type: Swiss Emmental, Swiss or French Gruyère, or
*   Norwegian Jarlsberg*
A spiced or herbed cheese: Leiden, Kuminost, or Dill Havarti
A blue-veined cheese, preferably one of the classics: Roquefort, Gorgonzola,
*   or Stilton, or a good domestic such as Maytag or Oregon Blue*
A strong, washed-rind ripened cheese: imported Muenster, Pont l'Evêque,
*   Esrom, or various strong monastery types*
A firm to hard Dutch cheese: Edam or Gouda
A mellow, semisoft to firm cheese: Italian Fontina or Fontal, or French Port
*   Salut*

❁

An assortment of crackers and breads, both plain (water biscuits, matzos)
*   and whole-grain (Scandinavian-style rye crisps, pumpernickel, slightly*
*   sweet wheat meal biscuits)*
Unsalted butter (optional)
Apples, pears, or grapes
Prepared mustard
Gherkins or pickle spears
Chutney or whole cranberry sauce
Radishes, celery sticks

Cheese for Dessert

After a meal, two ounces of cheese per person should do. A single cheese may be enough, and two or three selections is plenty. Skip the savory accompaniments in the recipe and stick to crackers, breads, and fruit, perhaps adding some walnuts.

Be sure to allow time for the cheeses to come to room temperature before serving. Arrange them on cutting boards or platters. If possible, have a separate knife or spreader for each cheese, suitable to the texture of the cheese: slicers for the firmer cheeses, broad knives for softer or crumbly types. Small individual plates are handy if you are serving several cheeses.

Holiday Wassail Bowl

Wassail, a sweetened and spiced punch made with ale, wine, or both, is a traditional English drink at Christmas and Twelfth Night. I developed this recipe a few years ago for Bruce Cost's book *Ginger: East to West.* According to Bruce, wassail has its roots in medieval medicinal brews, and the name comes from a toast to health.

Serves 24

12 tart cooking apples
¼ cup brown sugar
4 bottles Stout
4 bottles Pale Ale or lager
1 fifth medium sherry
½ teaspoon grated nutmeg
½ teaspoon cardamom seeds
3 cloves
3 whole allspice
1 cinnamon stick, crumbled
2 teaspoons ground ginger
Zest of 2 lemons
12 eggs
½ cup sugar

1. Preheat the oven to 300°. Core the apples, leaving the bottoms intact. Put a teaspoon of brown sugar in each cavity, place the apples in a buttered baking dish, and bake until soft, about 30 minutes. (This may be done ahead of time; keep the apples warm.)

2. Combine the ales and sherry in a large kettle and add the spices and lemon zest. Bring almost to a boil, stirring occasionally to release the foam from the ale, and simmer 5 minutes. Meanwhile, separate the eggs. Place the yolks in a large punch bowl and beat them lightly. In a separate bowl, beat the whites to soft peaks, add the sugar, and continue beating until stiff but not dry. Fold the whites into the yolks in the punch bowl. Strain the hot ale mixture into the bowl, beating constantly. Add the baked apples. Serve the punch in small cups; the apples can also be eaten.

The Original Eggnog?

According to the Oxford English Dictionary, eggnog was a warm drink based on beer, cider, wine, or spirits long before it evolved into its current form, a cold drink made with milk. "Nog" is an old word in East Anglia for a kind of strong ale.

Rice Pudding with Stout

This flavorful pudding is a fine party buffet dish as well as a satisfying warm dessert for an afternoon get-together in cool weather. Pop it in the oven a half hour before the football game starts and it will be ready to eat at halftime. Of course, you can also serve it as dessert after dinner. Time it to come out of the oven as you're sitting down to eat, and it will be the perfect serving temperature by dessert time.

Serves 8

> 1 cup medium-grain rice, such as Calrose
> 2 cups water
> ¾ teaspoon salt
> 1 tablespoon unsalted butter, plus more for the baking dish
> 1 tablespoon (approximately) fine bread crumbs
> 4 large eggs
> 1 cup sweet Stout (see Note)
> 1 cup whipping cream
> ½ teaspoon vanilla extract
> 1 tablespoon sugar
> ¼ teaspoon **each** cinnamon and nutmeg
> ⅛ teaspoon ground cloves
> ¼ pound pitted dates, chopped (about ⅔ cup)
> 2 tablespoons (approximately) all-purpose flour

1. Combine the rice, water, and salt in a heavy saucepan. Bring to a boil, reduce the heat, cover, and cook until the water is absorbed, about 15 minutes. Remove from the heat, fluff with a fork, cover, and let cool.

2. Butter the bottom and sides of a 6-cup baking dish or 8 individual casseroles. Sprinkle in the bread crumbs and roll the dish around to coat all the surface with crumbs. Tap out the excess.

3. Preheat the oven to 325°. Beat the eggs lightly in a large bowl. Add the Stout, ⅓ cup of the cream, vanilla, sugar, and spices and stir to combine. Add the rice and stir to break up any clumps. Toss the dates in flour to coat them evenly, shaking off the excess, and stir them in. Pour the mixture into the baking dish. Cut the butter into small pieces and scatter them on top. Bake uncovered until set, about 1 hour. Serve warm, with the rest of the cream, lightly whipped.

NOTE A sweet Stout in the English style (including those labeled Oatmeal Stout, Milk Stout, or Imperial Stout) will provide a mellow richness and overtones of coffee and chocolate, but a dry Irish-style Stout is likely to be too bitter. Some brands of Porter might also work, if on the sweet side.

"St. George he was for England,
And before he killed the dragon
He drank a pint of English ale
Out of an English flagon."
— G. K. Chesterton
The Englishman

45

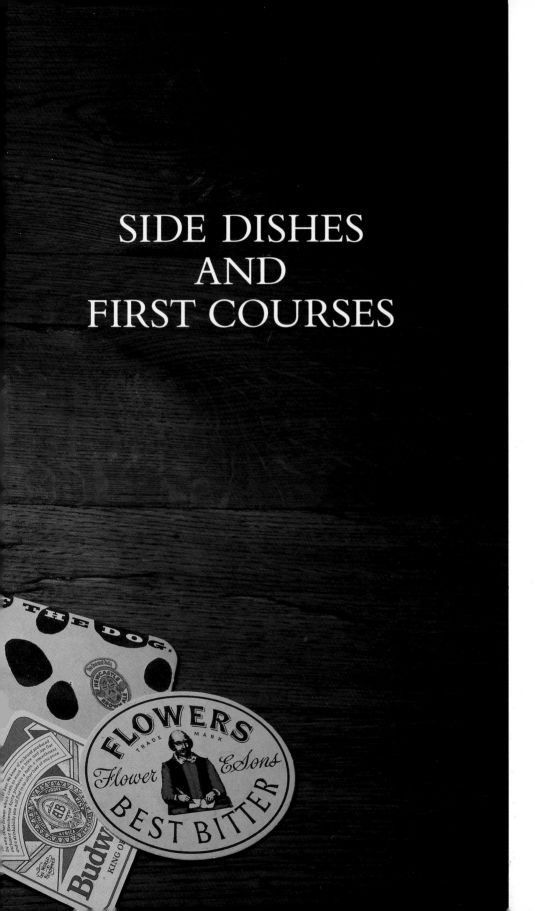

SIDE DISHES
AND
FIRST COURSES

Shrimp Ball Soup
    with Chipotle Chiles
Smoked Turkey Gumbo
Beer-Steamed Clams
Chupe de Elote y Papas
Fried Okra
Beer Biscuits
Skillet Cornbread
Risotto with Ham and Peas
Fettuccine with Smoked Fish
    and Sweet Corn
Spaghetti alla Puttanesca
Smoked Chicken
    and Arugula Salad
Warm Salad
    with Sausage and Fennel

Beer-Steamed Clams
(recipe, pg. 51)

Shrimp Ball Soup with Chipotle Chiles

The first sip of this soup packs a considerable punch from smoky *chipotle* chiles. Once the heat subsides a bit (I recommend a sip of cold Mexican lager) you will find yourself drawn back for another taste and another. This recipe is based on the crab soup typical of the northeast coast of Mexico; it would also work well with flaked cooked crabmeat in place of the shrimp balls. Or you could use plain peeled and deveined shrimp, but it wouldn't be as much fun.

Serves 4 to 6

> 2 large or 3 medium tomatoes
> 2 cloves garlic
> 2½ tablespoons oil
> 1 pound small or medium raw shrimp, peeled and deveined, shells reserved
> 3 medium green onions, white parts sliced, tops reserved
> 1 quart water
> Salt, to taste
> 2 dried or canned chipotle chiles (see left)
> Lime or lemon wedges
> Dried oregano leaves or fresh cilantro sprigs

1. Put the tomatoes and garlic in a shallow pan or a tray fashioned from heavy-duty aluminum foil. Broil, turning as necessary, until the tomato skins are well browned all over, about 5 minutes. Peel and mince the garlic and set it aside. Let the tomatoes cool slightly, then peel and chop them. Set the chopped tomatoes aside, reserving the skins and any juices in the pan.

2. Heat 1½ tablespoons of the oil in a large saucepan over medium heat. Add the shrimp shells and green onion tops and cook, stirring, until the shells turn pink, about 2 minutes. Add the water and the tomato skins and juice. Bring to a boil, reduce the heat, and simmer 10 minutes.

3. Sprinkle the shrimp with a little salt and chop them as finely as possible by hand or by pulsing them in a food processor. With moistened hands, form the shrimp into 1-inch balls.

4. Strain the simmered broth and set it aside. Wipe the pan dry, return it to the heat, and add 1 tablespoon of oil. Add the garlic and sliced green onions and cook until fragrant, about 15 seconds. Add the broth, chopped tomatoes, and chiles and simmer until the chile flavor permeates the broth, about 2 minutes. Taste for seasoning, then add the shrimp balls. Cook 4 minutes and serve, with lime or lemon wedges and oregano or cilantro for seasoning each bowl to taste.

Fire & Smoke

Chile chipotle is the ripened and smoke-dried form of the familiar jalapeño chile. It is sometimes available dried, but is more often found in small cans, packed in a vinegar-based sauce (*adobo*). The chiles are intended just to flavor the broth; biting into a whole chipotle is not for the timid.

Smoked Turkey Gumbo

Smoking in a covered barbecue has become one of the most popular ways to cook a whole turkey; in fact, it's the standard method of cooking the holiday bird in many families. Here's a way to take advantage of all the flavor left in the carcass, as well as some of the leftover meat. The smoky stock eliminates the need for ham, sausage, or other smoked meats which often flavor a gumbo (and cuts out a bit of the fat as well).

Serves 6 to 8

> *Carcass from 1 smoked turkey, including any skin*
> *10 cups water (approximately)*
> *1 onion, sliced*
> *1 stalk celery, sliced*
> *3 sprigs parsley*
> *1 sprig fresh thyme or ¼ teaspoon dried thyme*
> *1 bay leaf*
> *¼ cup vegetable oil*
> *¼ cup all-purpose flour*
> *½ cup each finely diced onion, celery, and green or red bell pepper*
> *1 teaspoon New Mexico, California, or ancho chile powder*
> *½ teaspoon salt*
> *¼ teaspoon pepper*
> *¼ teaspoon each dried thyme and oregano, crumbled*
> *⅛ teaspoon cayenne (optional)*
> *2 cups shredded smoked turkey meat*
> *1 pound raw shrimp, peeled and deveined*
> *2 cups cooked long-grain rice*

1. Break up the turkey carcass if necessary to fit your stockpot. Add water to cover. Bring to a boil, reduce to a simmer, and skim off any foam that comes to the surface. Add the sliced onion, celery, parsley, thyme sprig, and bay leaf and simmer uncovered, skimming occasionally, for 2 to 4 hours. (The longer you cook it, the richer the stock will be.) Do not let the stock boil or it will turn cloudy.

2. In a large, heavy skillet (preferably cast iron), heat the oil over medium heat. Stir in the flour and cook, stirring and scraping the entire bottom of the pan at least every 10 seconds, until the resulting roux cooks to a deep mahogany color, 10 to 15 minutes. Adjust the heat as necessary to prevent scorching, which can give a bitter taste. Turn off the heat and continue stirring a minute or 2 until the mixture no longer gets darker on the bottom. Carefully stir in the diced vegetables; don't let the roux

BEER NOTE In the South, gumbo would be served with an ice-cold, pale lager. I prefer this dish with something with a little more body and richness — a Pale Ale or an amber lager, domestic or imported.

splatter—it can cause nasty burns. Stir to coat the vegetables evenly with roux, stir in the chile powder, salt, pepper, herbs, and cayenne, and set aside. (The roux can be prepared to this point while the stock cooks.)

3. Strain the stock, let it stand until the fat rises to the top, and skim off the fat. Bring 8 cups of the stock to a boil in a large pot, stir in the roux and vegetable mixture and the shredded turkey, and simmer until slightly thickened, about 15 minutes. Add the shrimp and simmer just until done, about 5 minutes. Taste for seasoning and correct if necessary. Serve in soup bowls over small scoops of rice.

VARIATION This recipe also works with smoked chicken. Remove the meat from 1 smoked chicken and shred 2 cups. (Reserve the rest of the meat for another use, such as the Smoked Chicken and Arugula Salad on page 61.) Make the stock with the carcass plus 2 to 3 pounds of additional chicken backs, necks, etc. Because you are starting with raw poultry rather than cooked, there will be more foam to skim off the stock in step 1.

Beer-Steamed Clams

This recipe will work with any small hard-shell clams, including true Little Necks from the East Coast, "littlenecks" or Manila clams from the Pacific Northwest, or New Zealand cockles. It's also great with mussels, or with the Eastern soft-shell clams known simply as steamers, although the latter have a tough membrane covering the shell opening and foot that needs to be peeled off before eating.

Serves 2

> *16 to 24 small live clams (1 to 1½ pounds)*
> *½ bottle beer*
> *6 to 8 slices fresh ginger*
> *2 green onions or shallots, sliced*
> *1½ tablespoons unsalted butter (room temperature, optional)*
> *French bread*

Scrub the clams well, discarding any open ones that do not close when handled. Place them in a saucepan with the beer, ginger, and green onions. Cover, bring to a boil, and cook until most of the shells are open, 3 to 5 minutes depending on the variety. Transfer the open clams to a serving bowl and cook the rest another minute or two. If they do not open, discard them. Swirl the butter into the broth and pour it over the clams. Serve with crusty bread for dunking in the broth.

BEER NOTE For cooking, use a beer that is not too bitter—standard American lagers are fine. Serve with a fine Pilsner or your favorite lager.

Chupe de Elote y Papas
(Peruvian Corn and Potato Stew)

Chupe is a Peruvian specialty, a chowderlike soup usually containing shrimp and other seafood. This is an all-vegetable version, concentrating on three of South America's greatest contributions to world gastronomy: potatoes, corn, and capsicum (chile peppers, represented here by cayenne and paprika). I like to serve it as a vegetable first course before a simple meat or poultry dish, or on its own as a light supper or lunch. It's perfectly all right to pick up the wheels of corn in your fingers and nibble at the kernels. In fact, according to the owner of an Andean restaurant where I first tasted the dish, the name *chupe* comes from a local dialect verb meaning to lick one's fingers. If you want to be a little more formal, impale the center of the cob with a fork.

Serves 4

> 1 tablespoon butter or oil
> ½ cup finely diced onion (½ medium onion)
> 2 cloves garlic, minced
> ¾ teaspoon sweet paprika
> ⅛ teaspoon cayenne
> 1⅓ cups milk
> ½ cup unsalted chicken stock or water
> 1 large thin-skinned potato, scrubbed and cut into large dice (about 1½ cups)
> 2 ears sweet corn, shucked and sliced into ¾-inch-thick rounds
> Salt, to taste

Melt the butter in a large saucepan over medium heat. Add the onion and garlic and cook until the onion softens. Add the paprika and cayenne and cook, stirring, until the onions are evenly stained red. Add the milk, stock, potato, corn, and a large pinch of salt. Bring almost to a boil, reduce the heat to low, cover, and simmer, stirring occasionally so the vegetables cook evenly, until the potatoes are tender, about 30 minutes. Taste for seasoning and adjust if necessary. Serve in soup bowls.

VARIATION For a main dish or a more substantial side dish, add peeled and deveined raw shrimp and/or cleaned and sliced squid during the last 5 minutes of cooking.

BEER NOTE This is good with every-day lager, but a richer amber lager or ale is a better match for the creamy richness of the soup.

Chupe de Elote y Papas, variation with shrimp

Fried Okra

If you think you don't like okra, try it this way. Crunchy, bright green, and not the least bit slimy, it's a good side dish with simple roasted or barbecued meats, and a good nibble before dinner.

Serves 4

> *Oil for deep-frying*
> *1 pound small fresh okra, in 1-centimeter-thick slices (see Note)*
> *½ cup corn meal*
> *Salt and pepper, to taste*

Pour 1½ inches of oil into a wok or deep skillet. Heat it to 350° and adjust the heat to low. A handful at a time, toss the okra in the corn meal and shake off the excess. Fry until golden brown, about 1 minute. Retrieve the slices with a wire skimmer, drain them briefly over the oil, then drain on paper towels. Season to taste after cooking. Serve hot.

VARIATION If you really can't stand the idea of okra, try rounds of zucchini or other summer squash fried in the same way.

NOTE This admittedly unusual thickness, slightly more than ⅜ inch, is just perfect for producing okra slices that come out fully cooked without the corn meal getting too brown.

Beer Biscuits

Replacing the usual milk or buttermilk with beer gives these biscuits an especially light texture. They have a powerful beery aroma when they come out of the oven, but it dissipates quickly, leaving only a hint of beer flavor.

Makes 1 dozen 2½-inch biscuits

> *2 cups all-purpose flour*
> *2½ teaspoons baking powder*
> *¾ teaspoon salt*
> *3 tablespoons each butter and vegetable shortening, well chilled*
> *⅔ cup flat beer (room temperature)*

1. Preheat the oven to 400°. Mix the dry ingredients thoroughly in a medium bowl. Cut the butter and shortening into small pieces and add them. With a pastry blender, two table knives, an electric mixer, or by rubbing the mixture together with your fingertips, blend the flour and

fat until the mixture resembles coarse meal. Make a well in the center and pour in the beer. Stir just until the mixture is evenly moistened, then turn it out onto a lightly floured surface.

2. Knead just until the dough comes together, about 30 seconds. Roll it out with a rolling pin to a thickness of about ½ inch. Cut out biscuits with a 2½-inch round cutter (a wine glass works well) dipped in flour. Push straight down with the cutter and wiggle rather than twisting it to loosen the biscuits. You should get 8 or 9 biscuits out of the first rolling of the dough.

3. Lift away the trimmings and transfer the biscuits to an ungreased baking sheet. Gently press the trimmings together, overlapping them slightly, and roll the dough out again to ½ inch thick; cut the remaining biscuits. Discard the trimmings. Bake the biscuits until golden brown, 12 to 15 minutes. Serve hot.

Skillet Cornbread

If you like your cornbread the way I do, with a crunchy bottom crust, try baking it in a preheated cast-iron skillet. If you prefer it a little more tender on the bottom, use an 8- by 10-inch baking pan and skip the preheating step.

Makes 1 10-inch cornbread

> 6 tablespoons unsalted butter
> 1 cup yellow corn meal
> 1 cup all-purpose flour
> 2 teaspoons baking powder
> ½ teaspoon baking soda
> ½ teaspoon salt
> 1 cup buttermilk
> 1 large egg

1. Preheat the oven to 425°. Cut the butter into small pieces, put them in a 10-inch heavy cast-iron skillet, and place it in the oven while it warms.

2. Mix the dry ingredients together well in a large bowl. Combine the buttermilk and egg in another bowl and beat lightly. Stir in the melted butter from the skillet, then pour the mixture over the dry ingredients. Mix until well blended. Spread the batter in the skillet and bake until a knife inserted in the center comes out clean, 18 to 20 minutes. Serve warm.

CHEESE CORNBREAD Reduce the butter to 3 tablespoons and stir ¼ cup grated sharp cheddar cheese into the batter.

FRESH CORNBREAD Add ½ cup fresh or frozen corn kernels to the batter.

GREEN CHILE CORNBREAD Add 1 cup (or one 7-ounce can) diced roasted and peeled green chiles to the batter. Canned chiles are okay, but freshly roasted poblano chiles are better.

55

Risotto with Ham and Peas

Risotto is an Italian rice dish that is completely different from the way most Americans prepare rice. Instead of producing fluffy individual grains, the rice in risotto becomes creamy, although the center of each grain stays pleasantly firm, as it absorbs the flavorful cooking liquid.

A little beer in the cooking liquid gives an unusual flavor to this version, which can be served Italian-style as a first course or American-style alongside an entree. Use a beer that is not too bitter, such as Mexico's Dos Equis or Newcastle Brown Ale.

Serves 4 to 6

> *4 cups hot chicken or beef stock (preferably homemade)*
> *2 tablespoons mild olive oil*
> *2 tablespoons minced shallot or yellow onion*
> *1⅓ cups Arborio or similar short-grain rice*
> *½ cup mild amber beer or ale (room temperature)*
> *½ teaspoon salt (omit if using canned broth)*
> *Freshly ground pepper, to taste*
> *¼ pound Black Forest-style ham, finely diced (to pea size)*
> *1 cup fresh or frozen peas*
> *½ cup grated Parmesan or aged Asiago cheese*

1. Have the stock simmering in a saucepan and a good-sized ladle handy. Combine the oil and shallot in a medium saucepan or deep skillet. Heat over medium heat until the shallot begins to sizzle, then stir in the rice. Cook 2 minutes, stirring constantly to coat the grains with oil.

2. Add the beer to the rice, stir to release the foam, and stir in enough stock to just cover the rice (about 1 cup). Add the salt and pepper and cook over medium-low heat, stirring occasionally, until the rice has absorbed most of the liquid. Add the ham and enough stock to cover the rice again. Continue cooking, stirring occasionally, until the liquid is absorbed, then taste a grain of rice. There should be a bit of raw, chalky center at this point. (If the rice tastes nearly done, skip or reduce the amount of stock in the next addition.) Cover the rice with stock again and add the peas. Continue cooking until the rice is done but still firm in the very center and the liquid has reduced to a creamy, clingy consistency. If the mixture begins to dry before the rice is done, add a little more stock.

3. Correct the seasoning, stir in half the cheese, and serve immediately, passing the rest of the cheese at the table.

California Risotto?

Risotto purists may howl at the suggestion, but I find that California medium-grain rice (Calrose or some similarly named variety) makes a risotto that is about 90 percent as good as Arborio at about 20 percent of the price.

VARIATION Snow peas or sugar snap peas cut into bite-size pieces can be substituted for the peas.

NOTE There are many variables that affect the cooking of risotto: the size and shape of the pan, the amount of liquid added each time, even the age of the rice. With experience you will develop a feel for varying amounts slightly to turn out a perfect risotto every time.

Fettuccine with Smoked Fish and Sweet Corn

Sweet summer corn and smoked fish is one of my favorite combinations. This dish looks best with yellow corn, but if a white variety tastes better, I would opt for flavor over color. Although any hot-smoked fish will work (trout, salmon, or albacore, to name a few), I like the rich, satiny smoked "black cod" (sablefish) of the Pacific Northwest best. Serve this rich dish with a fine Pilsner and follow it with a plain roast chicken or turkey, or the Charcoal-Roasted Pork Loin on page 110.

Serves 4

> *2 ears sweet corn (to yield about 2 cups kernels)*
> *1 tablespoon butter*
> *¼ cup sliced green onions*
> *Pinch of red pepper flakes*
> *1 cup whipping cream*
> *¼ pound hot-smoked fish, broken into small pieces*
> *¾ pound fresh fettuccine*
> *Salt and white pepper, to taste*

Have a large pot of boiling salted water ready to cook the pasta. Cut the corn kernels from the ears, cutting close enough to get most of the kernel but leaving the bases attached to the cob. Melt the butter in a large skillet over medium heat; add the green onions and red pepper flakes and cook 30 seconds. Add the corn and cook until heated through, about 2 minutes. Add the cream and smoked fish to the skillet and bring it to a boil; while waiting for it to boil, start cooking the pasta. Boil the sauce until slightly reduced; season to taste with salt and pepper. Drain the pasta as soon as it is cooked, add it to the skillet, and toss to coat it with the sauce. Serve immediately on warm plates, arranging the corn and fish on top.

*A Summer Menu
from the Grill*
Garlic Prawns Grilled in Foil
Fettuccine with Smoked Fish and Sweet Corn
Spaten Franziskaner Hefe-Weissbier
Grilled Duck Breasts with Sichuan Peppercorns
Anchor Steam Beer

Spaghetti alla Puttanesca

The spicy "harlot's style" tomato sauce in this dish supposedly originated among the prostitutes of Rome. Maybe because it can be stirred up in a hurry. Or maybe the wafting aromas of garlic, hot peppers, and other tangy ingredients drew potential customers who could then be tempted by other pleasures. Anyway, it's delicious, and it goes especially well with cold beer.

Serves 4

> ½ *pound spaghetti or other long, thin dried pasta*
> 2 *tablespoons olive oil*
> 1 *large clove garlic, minced*
> ¼ *teaspoon red pepper flakes, or to taste*
> 2 *anchovy filets, chopped*
> 1 *pound tomatoes, peeled, seeded, and chopped, with their juice*
> 2 *tablespoons chopped green olives*
> 1 *tablespoon capers*

Start the pasta cooking in abundant salted water. While it cooks, heat the oil in a large skillet over medium heat and cook the garlic, red pepper, and anchovy until fragrant. Add the tomatoes, olives, and capers and cook, stirring, until the sauce is slightly reduced. Taste for seasoning and adjust if necessary. Drain the cooked pasta and toss it in the sauce, either in the skillet or in a serving bowl. Serve immediately.

NOTE Don't drain the capers and olives too thoroughly, and please don't rinse them. A little bit of the pickling brine from the jar adds valuable flavor.

An Autumnal Italian Menu
Antipasto Platter
Spaghetti alla Puttanesca
St. Pauli Girl
Braised Lamb Shanks with Olives
Moretti "La Rossa" Doppio Malto
Pears, Grapes, and Fontina Cheese
Gösser Stiftsbräu

Smoked Chicken and Arugula Salad

This restaurant-style salad is easy to make at home. Smoked chickens are available in many specialty shops. Their slightly salty, smoke-infused meat goes perfectly with sweet roasted peppers and bitter, peppery arugula. If the peppers are roasted over a charcoal fire, they'll taste even better. Serve with a fine Pilsner or Pale Ale.

Serves 4

> ¼ *cup slivered almonds*
> 1½ *teaspoons vinegar (sherry or red wine)*
> *Pinch of salt*
> *Freshly ground pepper, to taste*
> 2 *tablespoons olive oil*
> 1 *large bunch arugula (rocket, roquette) or watercress, washed, large stems removed, spun dry*
> 1 *cup shredded smoked chicken (approximately ¼ of a chicken)*
> 1 *large red bell pepper or pimiento, roasted, peeled, and cut into 2-inch-long strips*

1. Toast the almonds to a light golden brown in a small, dry skillet, shaking or stirring constantly so they do not scorch. Let cool.

2. In a large mixing bowl or salad bowl, combine the vinegar, salt, and pepper and stir until the salt dissolves. Add the oil and stir vigorously to emulsify the oil and vinegar. Add the arugula, chicken, and peppers and toss to coat everything evenly with dressing. Serve onto plates, arranging some of the chicken and peppers on top, and scatter almonds over all.

Roasting and Peeling Peppers

There are various methods for roasting sweet or hot peppers, all of them designed to remove the waxy outer skin as well as adding a roasted flavor to the flesh. Use whichever is most convenient.

A *charcoal fire* will give the most aromatic results. Whenever you have a fire going is a perfect time to roast some peppers for later use. Place the whole peppers directly on the grill over the hottest part of the fire and cook, turning occasionally, until the skin is blistered and beginning to blacken all over, but not so long in any one spot that the flesh underneath burns. You can do the same thing under an *oven broiler* or, if you have some way of supporting the peppers, directly over a *gas or electric range*. A *propane torch* also does the job, and you can concentrate the heat just where you want it. Once the peppers are blistered all over, transfer them to a large jar or bowl, cover, and let them steam in their own heat for 15 minutes. The skins should then slip away easily. Paper towels are handy for rubbing off small bits of skin. Slit open the peppers and discard the seeds and ribs, but save the sweet juices inside the pepper.

There is another, somewhat easier method that produces a more cooked texture: Simply bake the whole peppers in a *350° oven* for an hour, then turn off the heat and let them cool. (They can sit overnight in the turned-off oven.) The skins will slip off easily, though the flavor will not be as intense.

Warm Salad with Sausage and Fennel

Warm salads have become extremely popular items on the menus of contemporary restaurants. By combining a small amount of meat with flavorful greens and garnishes, they turn a simple green salad into a wonderfully satisfying first course dish. Add some good bread and perhaps a cup of soup, and you have a fine lunch or light supper.

Serves 4

> *3 to 4 cups mixed salad greens (see Note)*
> *1 small bulb fresh fennel (sweet anise)*
> *¼ pound fresh or smoked sausage*
> *2 tablespoons olive oil*
> *2½ teaspoons wine vinegar*
> *Salt and freshly ground pepper, to taste*
> *2 tablespoons raisins or pomegranate seeds*

1. Tear the greens into bite-size pieces if necessary. Wash, spin dry, and set aside at room temperature. Trim off the green tops of the fennel; split the bulb lengthwise, then slice it thinly crosswise. Warm a large stainless or heatproof glass mixing bowl by running hot water in it; wipe it dry.

2. Slice or dice the smoked sausage, or remove the casing from the fresh sausage and tear it into small pieces. Cook the sausage in a skillet over medium heat, adding a tiny bit of oil if necessary, until cooked through and lightly browned.

3. Meanwhile, combine the vinegar with a pinch of salt and pepper in the mixing bowl (remember to allow for the seasoning in the sausage) and stir with your fingertips to dissolve the salt. Add the greens, fennel, and raisins and toss to moisten everything lightly with vinegar.

4. When the sausage is done, transfer it to the salad bowl with a slotted spoon. Discard all but about 1 teaspoon of the drippings from the pan and add the oil. Heat it quickly over high heat until sizzling hot, then pour it over the greens in the bowl. Immediately toss to coat everything with the warm oil, wilting the greens slightly. Taste for seasoning, correct if necessary, and serve on warmed plates, arranging some of the sausage, fennel, and raisins on top of each portion.

NOTE I like a mixture of greens for this salad, including some red radicchio, for both color and flavor, and some slightly bitter greens such as curly endive, escarole hearts, or baby red mustard. You may find these greens pre-mixed with milder lettuces in produce markets or supermarkets with salad bars.

Choosing Sausages

Sausages in all their variety are among the best foods to go with beer. Most of the recipes in this book which use sausage specify a particular type (fresh or fully cooked, smoked or not, fine-textured or coarse). In general, they are not interchangeable; if a recipe calls for a fine-textured, fully cooked variety it won't work with a coarsely ground raw sausage, and vice versa. Within a given category, however, feel free to experiment. I'm particularly fond of some of the newer varieties, both fresh and smoked, made from chicken, turkey, and duck.

This recipe is an exception; it will work with either fresh sausages or the coarser fully cooked types. The former should be sliced (or better yet, crumbled) and cooked first, while the latter can be cut into neat dice and simply reheated and browned slightly.

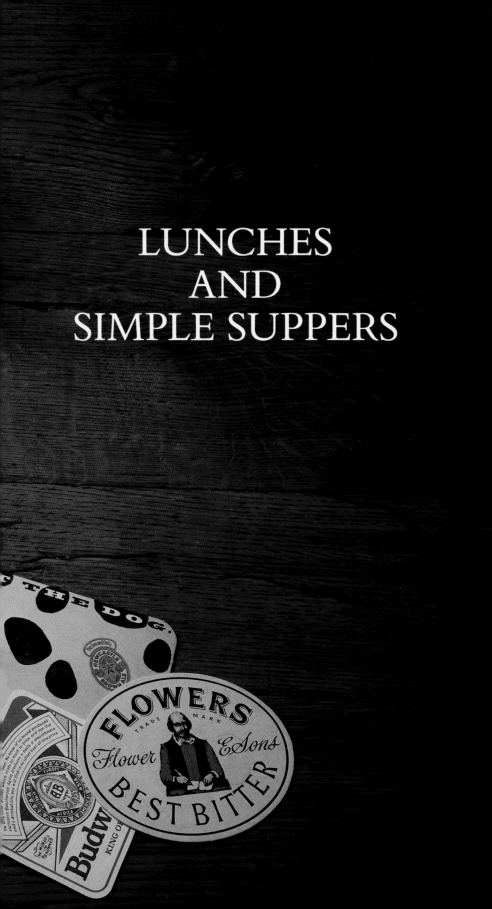

LUNCHES
AND
SIMPLE SUPPERS

Beer Batter Fish & Chips
Vegetable Masala Curry
Welsh Rabbit
Smothered Pork Chops
 with Apples
Reuben Sandwich à la Dijonnaise
Stir-Fried Squid and Noodles
 with Basil
Mango Chutney
Navy Beans and Cornbread
Braised Sausages and Polenta
Sausages with Braised Sauerkraut
Ham and Chicken Pot Pies
Turkey Mole Pot Pies
Two-Potato Hash
Rio Grande Chile-with-an-E

Reuben Sandwich à la Dijonnaise
(recipe, pg. 71)

Beer Batter Fish & Chips

Fish and chips is England's greatest contribution to the world of fast food. It also happens to be a good way to turn leftover beer into a valuable "secret" ingredient. A bit of beer in the batter gives it an extra lightness as well as a distinctive flavor.

As simple as it may seem, making good fried fish and potatoes requires attention to detail in both ingredients and technique. Read the tips in the margin before you begin.

Serves 4

> *1 pound Kennebec or other frying potatoes, washed, unpeeled*
> *1 egg yolk, beaten*
> *½ cup flat beer*
> *½ teaspoon salt, plus more for sprinkling*
> *½ cup flour, plus more for dredging*
> *1 pound fish filets*
> *Oil for deep-frying*
> *Lemon wedges or malt vinegar*

1. *One to 24 hours ahead of serving,* cut the potatoes lengthwise into ⅜-inch-thick slices; stack the slices and cut them lengthwise into square sticks. Place the potatoes in a bowl and cover them with cold water; refrigerate if storing them for more than a few hours. Prepare the batter as follows: Combine the egg yolk, beer, and ½ teaspoon salt in a bowl and stir to dissolve the salt. Gradually add ½ cup of flour and stir with a whisk until smooth. Cover and refrigerate for at least 30 minutes. Rinse and dry the fish filets and cut them into pieces about 2 ounces each and no more than ¾ inch thick. Refrigerate until ready to cook.

2. *Thirty minutes to 4 hours ahead of serving,* fill a deep saucepan, wok, or automatic fryer with oil to a depth of several inches but no more than two-thirds full. Fix a frying thermometer to the pan so that you can easily read the temperature of the oil; heat it to 300° over high heat. Meanwhile, drain a handful or two of potatoes in a sieve or, better still, spin them dry in a salad spinner. Reduce the heat to medium and add the potatoes; stir once or twice with a skimmer. Watch the temperature and adjust the heat to keep it as close as possible to 300°. Fry the potatoes until they are beginning to brown and the surface looks blistery, 5 to 7 minutes. Remove them with the skimmer, drain them briefly, and set them aside in a heatproof bowl or baking dish. As soon as they are cool enough to taste, try one. It should be soft throughout, with no raw crispness in the center, but not browned crisp on the outside. If the

The Fish

Any lean, mild, white-fleshed fish will do. North Atlantic cod is the all-time favorite, but Pacific cod and other members of the cod family (pollock, haddock, New Zealand hoki, and southern hake or "Antarctic queen") are all good choices. Catfish and Pacific lingcod (unrelated to the true cods) also work very well, as do some smaller, more tender varieties of shark.

center is still raw, return the potatoes to the pan for a little longer. Cook the remaining potatoes in the same way. Turn off the heat under the oil until you are ready to finish the potatoes.

3. Preheat the oven to 200°; heat the oil to 375°. Fry the potatoes a handful or two at a time to a deep golden brown, about 5 minutes. Drain them thoroughly over the oil then place them on a paper-lined sheet pan, salt them lightly, and put them in the oven to keep warm.

4. Reduce the oil temperature slightly, to between 350° and 360° (use the higher temperature for thinner pieces of fish, lower for thicker). Dredge a few pieces of fish in flour and shake off the excess. Drop each piece into the batter to coat it evenly, then slide it into the hot oil. Cook until golden brown, 3 to 4 minutes. While the first few pieces are cooking, flour and batter the next. Keep an eye on the temperature and adjust it as necessary. Drain the cooked fish thoroughly and keep it warm in the oven while cooking the rest. Serve with malt vinegar (the traditional condiment, made from the same kind of malt used for brewing beer) or lemon (my preference).

VARIATION In the first stage of cooking (step 2), the potatoes can be parboiled instead of fried. This method is especially suited to drier, more mature baking potatoes. Cut and soak the potatoes as above. Bring 2 quarts of water and 2 teaspoons of salt to a boil in a saucepan. Drain the potatoes and boil half at a time until they begin to go limp and no longer taste raw in the center, about 6 to 7 minutes. Drain and cool to room temperature.

The Potatoes

The best potatoes for frying fall somewhere between "new" potatoes and "all-purpose" russets in moisture and sugar content. Kennebecs are the professional chef's choice, but this variety doesn't keep well, so they are seldom found in stores. The thinnest-skinned, least mature russets you can find are next best. In any case, the 2-step cooking method described in the recipe gives the perfect combination of a fluffy interior and crisp outside.

The Oil

The simple fact is you can't make great fried anything with mediocre oil. Treat yourself to a gallon can of peanut oil (it's likely to be cheapest at an Asian market). Don't let the oil get too hot in cooking. Carefully filter it through several layers of cheesecloth after each use and put it back in the can. (A coffee filter also works, but it is very slow.) You can fry fish in the same oil half a dozen or more times; discard it when it has darkened noticeably or has a burnt aroma.

Temperature Control

Temperature control is crucial to successful frying. This fish and chips recipe uses three different frying temperatures, none of which can afford a lot of leeway. A thermostatically controlled fryer is ideal, but you can do just as well with a frying thermometer clipped onto the side of the pan.

Vegetable Masala Curry

This fragrant, moderately hot curry makes a fine vegetarian main dish, or you can serve it as a side dish (for 4 to 6 people) to accompany meat or poultry. Blending your own spices rather than using prepared curry powder gives the dish a fresh brightness and lets you adjust the flavor to suit your personal taste.

Serves 2 or 3

   1 tablespoon clarified butter or vegetable oil
   1 cup diced onion
   2 teaspoons minced garlic
   1 tablespoon minced ginger
   ¼ teaspoon turmeric
   ½ teaspoon garam masala (see right)
   Seeds from 4 cardamom pods (heaping ¼ teaspoon)
   ⅛ to ¼ teaspoon cayenne
   1 cup unflavored yogurt (preferably without gelatin)
   ½ teaspoon salt
   1 small head cauliflower, cut into florets
   2 small red new potatoes, scrubbed and diced
   ½ cup peeled and diced carrot
   ½ cup peas
   Cooked long-grain rice (preferably Basmati)
   Toasted slivered almonds (optional)

Combine the clarified butter, onion, garlic, and ginger in a large, heavy casserole. Cook over medium-low heat until the onions begin to color, about 2 minutes. Stir in the turmeric, *garam masala,* cardamom, and cayenne and cook until the mixture is well stained, about 1 minute. Add the yogurt and salt and bring to a simmer. Add the cauliflower, potatoes, and carrots; cover and simmer until the vegetables are almost tender, about 20 minutes. Add the peas and continue cooking, stirring occasionally, until all the vegetables are done, about 5 minutes. Taste for seasoning and correct if necessary. Serve hot or warm, with long-grain rice (preferably Basmati or another fragrant variety). Garnish with toasted almonds, if desired.

GARAM MASALA The name garam masala literally means "hot spices," but none of the spices in this versatile blend is especially hot. You can buy it already blended in some spice shops, but it is easy to make at home with a spice grinder, and it will taste fresher. Just combine equal parts of black peppercorns, cardamom seeds, coriander seeds, and cumin seeds plus half portions of crumbled cinnamon stick and cloves and grind to a powder. Store garam masala tightly sealed in a jar and use it as a base for curries and other Indian dishes. Try to make no more than you will use in a month or two, as the flavor deteriorates after grinding.

Rabbit or rarebit? Whatever you call it, this dish of melted cheese on toast is a fine (and filling!) accompaniment to a good ale. Serve a salad alongside and follow it with a crunchy apple for lunch or supper.

Serves 6

½ cup Pale Ale or Porter
1 tablespoon prepared mustard
Dash of Worcestershire sauce
½ teaspoon paprika
Pinch of cayenne
½ pound sharp cheddar cheese, grated (about 2 cups)
2 teaspoons cornstarch
6 slices whole-grain bread, toasted

Combine the ale, mustard, Worcestershire sauce, paprika, and cayenne in a medium saucepan and heat it to just short of boiling. Toss the cheese with the cornstarch and add it to the pot. Stir and cook over low heat until smooth. Spoon the melted cheese over the toast, or keep it warm as a dip for cubes of bread, fondue style.

About the name

Whether it refers to an unsuccessful hunter, or to the fact that the best hunting grounds and all the game on them belonged to the aristocratic English landlords, the implication is clear that in Wales, melted cheese has often had to do when a meat dish would be preferred. (In a similar example, a certain scrambled egg dish has become known as Scotch woodcock.) At the risk of offending any Welsh readers, I quote the following from Fowler's *Modern English Usage*: "The etymologist is aware, and the person who has paid no attention to the subject is probably unaware, . . . that *Welsh rabbit* is amusing and right, *Welsh rarebit* stupid and wrong."

Smothered Pork Chops with Apples

Fruit and pork are traditional partners. The apples bring out the fruity aromas of a good dry-hopped ale.

Serves 4

4 thick rib-end pork chops, about 2 pounds in all
Salt and freshly ground black pepper
2 medium onions, sliced
1 clove garlic, sliced
½ teaspoon caraway seeds
1 cup chicken or veal stock
2 tart apples, cored and cut into eighths

1. Trim any excess fat from the chops and season them lightly on all sides with salt and pepper. Heat a deep heavy skillet or dutch oven over medium heat and rub it with a piece of pork fat. Add the chops and brown them well on both sides. Set them aside. Add the onions and garlic to the skillet and cook, stirring, until the onions are soft. Add the caraway seeds and stock and bring to a boil. Reduce the heat and return

the chops to the pan. Cover and simmer 20 minutes. Add the apples and continue cooking until the chops are tender, another 20 to 30 minutes. Regulate the heat so the liquid just simmers.

2. Transfer the chops to a platter or individual plates and top them with the apples and onions. Raise the heat to high and reduce the sauce in the pan by a third. Taste it for seasoning and adjust if necessary. Spoon the sauce over the chops and serve.

Reuben Sandwich à la Dijonnaise

The classic Reuben combines corned beef, Swiss cheese, sauerkraut, and Russian dressing in a grilled sandwich. The Russian dressing never made sense to me. It's too sweet and makes the whole thing too gooey, so I leave it out and use good mustard instead. Buy real Swiss or French Gruyère, not domestic "swiss"; it makes all the difference.

Makes 1 sandwich

> *2 slices rye bread*
> *Dijon or other full-flavored mustard*
> *1 ounce sliced Gruyère cheese*
> *2 to 2½ ounces sliced corned beef*
> *¼ cup cold-pack sauerkraut, drained (see Note)*
> *Butter*

Spread both slices of bread with mustard. Top one with cheese, then corned beef, then sauerkraut, then the other slice of bread. Lightly butter the outside of the sandwich and cook it in a skillet or on a griddle over low heat until nicely browned on both sides. Serve warm with a Pilsner or other good pale lager.

NOTE The kind of sauerkraut sold in glass jars in the market's refrigerator section has a milder flavor than the canned version, and can be used straight from the jar. If using canned sauerkraut, you might wish to rinse off a bit of the brine.

Visions of Sauerkraut

A friend and I were backpacking in the Sierra Nevada during a college vacation. Late one afternoon we heard a passing hiker say, "A Reuben sandwich and a glass of beer sure would taste good right now." That thought tortured us for the rest of our trip. Days later when we got to Tuolumne Meadows, I called my girlfriend to come and meet us with a car. "And please," I said, "bring Reuben sandwiches and beer."

Stir-Fried Squid and Noodles with Basil

This dish combines Chinese cooking techniques (stir-frying and tossed noodle dishes) with some typically Thai ingredients. If you can get the purple-stemmed Thai basil also known as anise basil, it will give a more authentic flavor. Fresh mint is a good alternative to basil, and one that is equally at home in Thai and other Southeast Asian cuisines.

Serves 2

¼ pound fresh or dried Chinese-style thin egg noodles
¼ cup chicken stock
1 tablespoon lime or lemon juice
2 teaspoons fish sauce (see Note)
½ teaspoon sugar
2 tablespoons oil
2 teaspoons minced ginger
1 teaspoon minced garlic
2 or 3 fresh red or green chiles, seeded and cut into narrow strips
1 pound fresh or thawed squid, cleaned for stir-frying (see page 28)
½ cup (loosely packed) fresh basil leaves

1. Cook the noodles according to package directions; drain and rinse them with cold water to stop the cooking. (This may be done well ahead of time; toss the cooked noodles with a little oil if not using them right away.) Combine the stock, lime juice, fish sauce, and sugar in a small bowl; stir to dissolve the sugar.

2. Heat 1 tablespoon of the oil in a wok or large skillet over high heat. Add the ginger, garlic, and chile strips and cook until fragrant, about 10 seconds. Add the squid and stir-fry until it turns opaque and curls up, about 45 seconds. Remove the contents of the wok to a plate and set aside.

3. Return the wok to the heat. Add another tablespoon of oil around the edge of the wok, letting it slide down the sides. Scatter the noodles in the pan, pulling apart any clumps. Cook 1 minute, then stir and scrape the noodles loose from the sides of the pan. Add the stock mixture, bring it to a boil, reduce it slightly, and add the squid mixture. Stir in the basil leaves and toss to combine everything well. Serve immediately, arranging some of the squid, chiles, and basil on top.

NOTE Fish sauce (*nam pla* or *nuoc mam*) is a salty brown liquid sauce used in many Southeast Asian cuisines the way soy sauce is used in Chinese and Japanese cooking, as a table condiment and cooking ingredient. I use the Thai variety sold in 24-ounce glass bottles in Asian markets.

MENU NOTE For a Southeast Asian meal, precede this with the Lamb Satay with Peanut Sauce on page 88. If you like, add a salad of shredded cabbage and cooked chicken or shrimp, dressed with a mixture of pounded chiles and garlic, lime juice, fish sauce, and a pinch of sugar. Singha beer from Thailand is especially appropriate with this kind of food, but any good international-style lager will do nicely.

Mango Chutney

This sweet and spicy chutney, similar to the famous Major Grey's variety, goes well with cold meats as well as Indian-style curries. It also makes a simple topping for crackers spread with cream cheese. It's an essential part of an English Ploughman's Lunch.

Makes 4 half-pints

> 3 large or 4 medium unripe mangoes (about 2½ pounds)
> 2 to 4 small dried chiles
> 1 cup cider vinegar
> 1½ cups sugar
> 1-inch cube fresh ginger, grated
> ½ cup seedless raisins, golden or black, chopped
> 1¼ teaspoons kosher salt
> ½ teaspoon **garam masala** (see page 69)
> ¼ teaspoon dry mustard

1. Wash the mangoes well and peel them with a peeler or a paring knife. Stand a mango up on its stem end; you will see that the fruit is slightly oval in cross-section (this varies by variety). Slice off one of the broad sides, then the other, leaving a slab in the center about ¾ inch thick around the pit. Carefully cut the rest of the meat off the pit in as large pieces as possible; stop when you reach the coarse fibers near the pit. Cut the two halves into ½-inch dice, and chop the miscellaneous pieces into smaller chunks. Slit the chiles open lengthwise and remove the seeds and ribs. Cut or break each chile into 2 or 3 pieces.

2. Combine the vinegar and sugar in a stainless or enameled saucepan and heat them until the sugar dissolves. Add the mango, chiles, and all the remaining ingredients. Bring the mixture to a boil, reduce the heat, and simmer until the chutney is quite thick and jammy, about 1½ hours. Transfer the chutney to clean, warmed glass jars; cover and refrigerate. For longer storage at room temperature, pack the chutney into half-pint canning jars and process them in a boiling water bath for 10 minutes, following the manufacturer's instructions.

NOTE Green (unripe) mangoes are best for making chutneys; they are sometimes sold in specialty markets. Otherwise, look for mangoes when they first appear in the market and pick the ones with the greenest skin and the firmest flesh, just the opposite of what you would look for in a mango to be eaten fresh. If all you can find is fully ripe mangoes and you want to make chutney anyway, add a green apple, peeled, cored, and finely chopped, to supply additional pectin.

PLOUGHMAN'S LUNCH This perennial favorite of British pubs is simplicity itself, and the perfect accompaniment to a pint of good ale. Simply arrange on a plate a wedge of sharp cheese (Cheddar, Cheshire, Caerphilly, or a similar type), a tart apple, some good, chewy whole-grain bread, and something pickled. The last may be pickled onions, Branston pickles (a brand of blended pickled vegetables in a brown sauce), or a chutney of the Major Grey's type (see the recipe at right for an easy homemade version).

"There is nothing which has yet been contrived by man by which so much happiness is produced as by a good tavern or inn."
— Samuel Johnson

Navy Beans and Cornbread

My parents grew up in Oklahoma City during the Depression, and a pot of beans cooked with a ham bone was a favorite, economical main dish in both their families. It was always served over cornbread, and the cornbread was never sweet. The dish remained a favorite, and our family enjoyed "Oklahoma cassoulet" (my name for it, not theirs) in all the places we lived—Long Island, the suburbs of Chicago, and the San Francisco Bay Area.

Because this is such a substantial dish, you don't need an especially heavy beer to go with it, just a good lager. Mustard, collard, or other slightly bitter greens are the traditional accompaniment, adding balance in color and nutrition as well as flavor. The beans are even better after cooling and reheating.

> *1 cup navy, Great Northern, or other small white beans*
> *1 meaty ham hock or shank, or a bone from a whole ham with some meat*
> *   still attached*
> *1 bay leaf*
> *Salt and pepper, to taste*
> *Skillet Cornbread (page 55)*

1. Sort through the beans and remove any bits of gravel or damaged beans. Place the beans in a bowl, add cold water to cover, and soak 8 hours to overnight. Drain and rinse the beans and transfer them to a large, heavy pot; add enough water to cover them by 1 inch. Bring the pot to a boil, reduce the heat, and add the ham hock and bay leaf. Cover and simmer until the beans are quite tender, about 1¼ hours. Season to taste. (Depending on the saltiness of the ham, you may not need any more salt.)

2. Prepare the cornbread. Time it to come out of the oven just before serving time. To serve, split a wedge of cornbread horizontally and spoon the beans and broth over it. Add chunks of meat pulled from the ham hock.

TECHNIQUE NOTE If you don't have time to soak the beans for 8 hours, use this quick soaking method: Bring the beans and water to a boil, cook 2 minutes, remove from the heat, and let stand 1 hour. Drain, rinse, and cook as above.

Bean Cuisine

Dishes made up of beans, smoked pork, and something starchy are found all over the Americas. Black-eyed peas are cooked and served in much the same way as these navy beans throughout the South. In northern Mexico and the American Southwest, pinto beans cooked with bacon become *frijoles charros* ("cowboy beans") and are served with corn tortillas. In Louisiana, it's Red Beans and Rice, small red beans cooked with plenty of sausage and the spicy ham known as tasso, then served in a bowl with rice. Around the Caribbean and southward, the beans are usually black, and when served with rice may be called *Moros y Cristianos* ("Moors and Christians"). The theme reaches its most elaborate form in *Feijoada,* the national dish of Brazil, which combines black beans with assorted smoked meats and greens and is served with both rice and toasted bits of cassava meal (a form of tapioca). All these dishes are great beer food, and go best with not-too-filling beers.

Braised Sausages and Polenta

This is a good way to serve uncooked, coarse-textured sausages, from the familiar Italian style to some of the newer versions such as chicken and apple or whiskey-fennel. Serve with a nice malty lager such as a Bavarian Märzen.

Serves 4

> *4 cups cold water*
> *1 cup polenta (coarse-ground corn meal)*
> *1 teaspoon salt*
> *1½ to 2 pounds Italian or other coarse uncooked sausages*
> *4 tablespoons minced celery*
> *2 tablespoons minced oil-packed sun-dried tomatoes*
> *2 tablespoons pine nuts, toasted and chopped*
> *1 tablespoon oil from dried tomatoes*
> *1 tablespoon chopped parsley*

1. Combine the water, polenta, and salt in a large, heavy saucepan. Stir to break up any lumps. Bring to a boil, reduce the heat to medium-low, and simmer, stirring frequently, until the grains taste done and the polenta is thick but still pourable, about 20 minutes. Remove from the heat and cover the pot until ready to serve; if keeping longer than the time it takes to cook the sausages, keep warm in a double boiler.

2. Puncture each sausage in a couple of places with a toothpick. Arrange the sausages in a single layer in a heavy skillet. Add water to a depth of about ¼ inch. Bring the water to a boil over high heat, reduce the heat to medium, cover, and steam 15 minutes. Remove the cover, turn the heat to medium-high, and cook until the water is gone and the sausages begin to sizzle and brown. (To reduce spattering, put the cover back on slightly ajar.)

3. Stir the remaining ingredients into the polenta, taste for seasoning, and correct if necessary. Spoon a large pool of polenta onto each plate and arrange a couple of sausages on top.

March in October?

One might expect that Märzenbier, or "March beer," is meant to be drunk in March. Not so. This Bavarian specialty beer is brewed in the spring and aged through the summer so as to be ready to be served at Oktoberfest.

Sausages with Braised Sauerkraut

This is not a classic Alsatian *choucroute garni,* meant to be served with white wine. For that dish, as Julia Child describes it, the sauerkraut must be drained and soaked "to remove all but a suggestion of its preserving brine." To beer lovers, that tangy, salty flavor is exactly the point of sauerkraut! Here, the sauerkraut gets a brief cooking, then serves as a bed for steaming sausages.

Serves 4

> *1 tablespoon oil, chicken fat, or bacon drippings*
> *1 small onion, sliced*
> *1 teaspoon dill seed*
> *2 bay leaves*
> *2 tablespoons gin*
> *2 cups sauerkraut, drained*
> *1½ pounds fine-textured cooked sausages (see Note)*
> *Rye or other whole-grain bread*
> *Mustard*

BEER NOTE Serve any full-flavored lager, pale or dark, as long as it is not too bitter. Again, it's hard to beat a Munich Oktoberfest or other *festbier* with sausages.

1. Combine the oil and onion in a wide, heavy pan or deep skillet. Cook over medium-low heat until the onion is translucent. Add the dill seed, bay leaves, and gin; bring to a boil, stir in the sauerkraut, cover, and cook 20 to 30 minutes. (The sauerkraut can be prepared to this point several hours ahead and removed from the heat.)

2. Pierce the skins of the sausages well, or slash them with a couple of shallow diagonal cuts. Add them to the pan with the sauerkraut, cover, and cook over medium heat until the sausages swell but do not burst, 10 to 12 minutes depending on size. Serve with rye bread or another whole-grain bread and mustard of your choice. Steamed new potatoes are another nice accompaniment.

NOTE Use your choice of fine-grained sausages: the white varieties known as bockwurst or weisswurst; knockwurst or its smoked counterpart, bratwurst; short, fat garlic sausages; or plain old hot dogs or "dinner franks." All of these are fully cooked, and plump up when reheated. You can cook an assortment if you like, and let everyone help himself to his favorites. Firmer, coarser sausages of the kielbasa type are not as suitable for this dish, nor are uncooked Italian-style sausages.

Ham and Chicken Pot Pies

Pot pies are real comfort food, perfect for family suppers on chilly evenings. This single-crust version combines mild chicken, salty ham, and tangy mustard. All it needs to complete the meal is a simple salad or vegetable side dish and your favorite beer.

Makes 4 single-serving pies

Pot Pie Topping
1⅔ cups all-purpose flour
2½ teaspoons baking powder
¾ teaspoon salt
Scant cup whipping cream

❀

3 tablespoons plus 1 teaspoon unsalted butter or margarine
1 cup diced onion
½ cup diced celery
3 tablespoons all-purpose flour
1½ cups unsalted chicken stock
1 teaspoon chopped fresh tarragon or ¼ teaspoon dried tarragon leaves
1 teaspoon prepared mustard (any type)
1½ cups (about ¾ pound) diced cooked chicken or turkey
⅓ pound any good ham, finely diced
Salt and freshly ground pepper, to taste

1. Prepare the topping as follows: Mix the dry ingredients well in a large bowl. Stir in the cream with a fork just until the mixture is evenly moistened; turn it by hand in the bowl until most of the floury bits are absorbed. Cover and let the dough rest for at least 15 minutes.

2. Melt 4 teaspoons of butter in a saucepan over medium heat. Add the onions and celery and cook until the onions soften; do not brown. Stir in the flour and cook 1 minute. Stir in the stock and tarragon and cook until well thickened. Stir in the mustard, then the chicken and ham. Season to taste with salt and pepper. Spoon the mixture into 4 individual bake-and-serve casseroles and set aside to cool.

3. Preheat the oven to 350°. Turn the dough out onto a lightly floured board and press it with the fingertips and the heels of your hands to between ⅛ and ¼ inch thick. Cut the dough in quarters and shape each quarter gently with your fingertips into a circle the size of a casserole, thinning it out a little more if necessary to fit. Top each casserole with dough, pressing it well against the edges to seal; trim any excess with your hands. Melt the remaining 2 tablespoons of butter and brush the

"Just as the differences between a chardonnay, a cabernet, and a port can illuminate a meal, so can the distinctions that set apart a wheat beer, pilsner, and imperial stout."
—Michael Jackson
in *American Brewer*, Spring 1990

tops with it; cut 3 or 4 small vents in each pie. Bake until the crusts are golden brown, 20 to 25 minutes. Serve hot or warm.

NOTE   Be careful not to overwork the dough. Any excess kneading, or trying to work in every last bit of flour, or even rolling with a rolling pin instead of pushing the dough out by hand will build up the gluten in the flour and result in a tough crust.

Turkey Mole Pot Pies

Here's a way to turn holiday turkey leftovers into a whole new dish that doesn't seem like leftovers at all. The filling for these individual pot pies is based on the classic Mexican *mole poblano,* a complex stew of chiles, seeds, spices, and a bit of chocolate. Cubes of winter squash provide a sweet, mellow counterpart to the spicy sauce, as well as balancing the richness of what would otherwise be a straight meat pie.

Serves 4

> *2 dried ancho chiles,* **or** *1 ancho and 1 mulato (see Note)*
> *1 dried pasilla chile (see Note)*
> *Boiling water*
> *2 whole cloves*
> *¼ teaspoon peppercorns*
> *⅛ teaspoon anise or fennel seeds*
> *⅛ teaspoon coriander seeds*
> *1-inch piece cinnamon stick, crumbled*

Pot Pie Topping
> *1⅔ cups all-purpose flour*
> *2½ teaspoons baking powder*
> *¾ teaspoon salt*
> *Scant cup whipping cream*
> ❀
> *2 tablespoons oil, lard, or rendered chicken fat*
> *1 cup diced onion*
> *1 large clove garlic, chopped*
> *¼ cup slivered almonds*
> *3 tablespoons raisins*
> *1 heaping tablespoon sesame tahini*
> *1 tablespoon unsweetened cocoa*
> *1½ cups turkey or chicken stock*
> *1 teaspoon salt, or to taste*

MENU NOTE If you want to stay with a Mexican theme, start with a pale, dry lager and light appetizer such as Ceviche (page 33) or slices of jicama dipped in chile powder and seasoned with a squeeze of lime. To accompany the mole pot pies, choose a rich amber or dark lager on the sweet side, such as Mexico's Negra Modelo, Dos Equis, or Noche Buena. (Sad to say, as of this writing the last is no longer being imported into the U.S., but let's hope we see it again in the future.) Most southern German dark lagers would be at home with this dish as well.

2 cups cooked turkey, diced or shredded
1 cup small cubes winter squash, steamed 5 minutes and lightly salted

1. Warm a large, heavy skillet over medium-low heat. Add the chiles and toast, turning occasionally, just until they become flexible. Slit them open, discard the stems, and remove and reserve the seeds. Tear the chiles into thin strips. Place them in a small bowl, add boiling water just to cover, and let them stand 1 hour to overnight. Toast the spices and 1 teaspoon of the reserved chile seeds until quite fragrant, transfer them to a spice grinder or a mortar, and grind them to a powder. (This step may be done ahead of time.)

2. Prepare the topping as directed in Step 1, page 79. Warm the oil or fat in the skillet over medium heat. Add ¼ cup of the onion and the garlic, almonds, and raisins; cook until the onions are golden, about 3 minutes, then transfer the mixture with a slotted spoon to a food processor or blender. Lift the chiles out of their soaking water and add them to the processor. Blend to a paste, adding a little of the soaking water if needed.

3. Add the remaining onion to the skillet, cook until it begins to soften, and stir in the spice mixture and the chile puree. Cook, stirring constantly, until the mixture is well colored by the chiles, about 3 minutes. Stir in the tahini and cocoa and add the stock and salt. Simmer until the oil begins to rise to the surface. Taste for seasoning and correct if necessary. If you like a hotter flavor, grind more of the reserved chile seeds and add them. Stir in the turkey and remove from the heat.

4. Preheat the oven to 350°. Divide the squash cubes among four individual casseroles and add the turkey mixture. Top and bake as directed in Step 3, page 79.

NOTE A well-balanced *mole poblano* should have several varieties of dried chile, each adding its nuances of flavor. Recipes for this dish vary widely, but most versions call for at least the three varieties listed here. *Chile ancho* is a reddish-brown, wrinkled, roughly triangular chile about 3 inches long. It's the dried equivalent of the fresh *chile poblano. Chile mulato* is similar in size and shape to *ancho,* but is more of a brownish-black and has a slightly different taste. *Chile pasilla* is very long and slender, and almost black in its dried form. The names can be especially confusing in California, where the *pasilla* is usually sold as *chile negro,* and *anchos* are as often as not labeled *pasilla.*

MENU NOTE Of course, *mole poblano* doesn't have to go into a pot pie. It's more typically served as a thick stew on a plate, with rice or tortillas on the side. It also makes a great enchilada filling.

Two-Potato Hash

An Unforgettable Hash

Despite its mundane image, hash can be a memorable dish. I know of one hash I will never forget. Several years ago, when I was working for the newly formed American Institute of Wine and Food, I was invited to lunch at the home of one of the Institute's founders, Julia Child. I'm not sure what I was expecting—something with a French name, surely—but what she served was hash. Needless to say, Julia's hash, made with good ham, perfectly browned, and topped with poached eggs, was delicious.

Sweet potatoes can be a delicious stand-in for white potatoes, as I discovered a few years ago when I wanted to make a hash but was short on "bakers." The red-skinned sweet potatoes sold as Garnet yams give a subtly sweet flavor to this hash, a nice balance to the salty corned beef. You also get four distinct textures—the meat, the slightly crunchy onions, the firmer white potatoes, and the softer sweet potatoes. Sauteed spinach, kale, or other greens tossed with a little vinegar make a nice contrasting side dish.

Serves 4

> 1 large russet potato (about ¾ pound)
> 1 medium Garnet yam (about ¾ pound)
> 1 medium onion
> ½ pound cooked corned beef (about 1½ cups diced)
> ¼ teaspoon pepper, or to taste
> 2 tablespoons oil

Peel both potatoes and cut them into ¼-inch dice; dice the onion and corned beef to the same size. Combine the diced ingredients in a bowl and stir in the pepper. Heat the oil in a 10-inch nonstick skillet over medium heat. Spread the hash mixture evenly in the skillet and cook until lightly browned on the bottom, about 10 minutes. Using a wide spatula, turn the mixture over in as large sections as possible. Cook another 10 minutes, then turn again, breaking up the crust and working the less-browned parts from the outside of the pan into the center. Gently press the hash into a cake and cook another 10 minutes. Serve hot or warm.

BEER NOTE Although the hash is only slightly sweet, in combination with a beer that is noticeably sweet it may prove too much of a good thing. I prefer a rather dry, hoppy Pale Ale or a European Pilsner.

VARIATION Other cooked meats make excellent hash, including roast beef and dark meat from chicken or turkey (especially smoked). Ham will work too, if it's not too sweet a cure. If your ham is on the sweet side, using all white potatoes will give a better balance. Cured meats such as ham and corned beef provide plenty of salt; if you use other meats you will probably need to add salt to the hash. You might also experiment with adding dried herbs such as savory, tarragon, or marjoram to a poultry or roast beef hash.

Rio Grande Chile-with-an-E

This falls somewhere between a Texas and a New Mexico version of *chili con carne*. The typical Texas version uses a blend of spices, with a heavy emphasis on cumin, and may include beans and tomatoes, while the New Mexico *carne en chile colorado* is a simpler dish of beef stewed in a thin red chile sauce. As in the New Mexico style, I prefer to serve the beans separately rather than mixed with the meat. Chopping the meat by hand gives a much better texture than ground meat can ever produce, and it's really no more difficult.

Serves 6

> 1 blade chuck steak or roast, 2 to 3 pounds with bones
> ¾ teaspoon cumin seed
> ½ teaspoon black peppercorns
> ½ teaspoon oregano
> 2 tablespoons oil or lard
> 1 cup finely diced onion
> 2 large cloves garlic, chopped
> 2 tablespoons pure New Mexico chile powder, or to taste (see Note)
> ½ teaspoon salt
> 1 tablespoon masa harina (corn tortilla flour)
> Corn tortillas
> Cooked pinto beans

1. Trim any easily removable fat from the meat and slash the membranes around the outer edge. Heat a deep 12-inch skillet over medium-high heat and rub it with a piece of fat until it is lightly greased. Add the meat and brown it well on both sides. Add 1 cup of water, cover the pan, reduce the heat, and simmer until the meat is quite tender, about 2 hours. Transfer the meat to a plate. Pour the liquid into a heatproof glass container; let it stand until the fat rises to the top and discard the fat.

2. Toast the cumin and peppercorns in a small dry skillet until fragrant. Add the oregano and toast a few seconds longer. Grind the mixture in a spice grinder.

3. Return the meat skillet to medium heat and add the oil or lard. Cook the onion and garlic until they are soft and beginning to brown, then sprinkle in the ground spices and 2 tablespoons of chile powder. Cook 1 minute, stirring constantly so the chile does not scorch. Add the meat broth and salt and cook at a simmer.

Chili or chile?

The Spanish name for the *Capsicum* plant and its fruits is spelled *chile,* but the most common English spelling is *chili.* Except when referring to the Texas dish, I use the Spanish spelling (which, by the way, the New Mexico state legislature has adopted as the only proper way to spell it).

4. Meanwhile, pull the meat from the bones and cut away any large pieces of fat. Chop the meat coarsely with a heavy knife or cleaver. Add the chopped meat to the skillet and stir in the *masa harina*. Simmer until the meat is reheated and the liquid thickens slightly. Taste for seasoning and adjust if necessary; if you add more chile powder, simmer at least 5 minutes longer to avoid a raw flavor. Serve the chile in soup bowls, with warm corn tortillas and a separate bowl of cooked pinto beans on the side.

NOTES Try any leftovers as a filling for enchiladas or tacos.

Pure chile (with an *e*) powder contains nothing but ground dried red chiles; the chili (with an *i*) powder sold in every supermarket in the U.S. is a blend which also includes cumin and oregano. Look in the Mexican foods section of supermarkets for bags of pure chile powder, which may be labeled *chile molido* (ground). New Mexico chile gives a pleasant, not-too-hot flavor; California chile is milder, and Mexican varieties such as *chile ancho* are generally hotter. Experiment with different varieties to suit your taste.

BEER NOTE Nothing too fancy here—your favorite domestic or Mexican lager is fine.

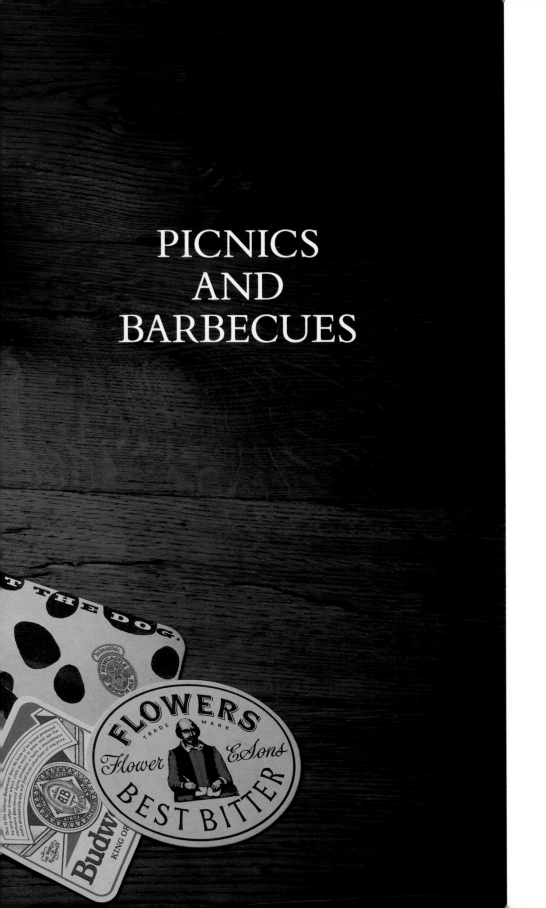

PICNICS
AND
BARBECUES

Lamb Satay with Peanut Sauce
Garlic Prawns Grilled in Foil
Barbecued Ribs with Plum Sauce
Grilled Shark with Assorted Salsas
Pistachio and
    Green Peppercorn Pâté
Grilled White Sausages
    with Red Chard
Grilled Fish with Mustard Glaze
Jerk Thighs
    (Jamaican Barbecued Chicken)
Elaine's Apple-Ginger Cake

Barbecued Ribs with Plum Sauce
(recipe, pg. 92)

It's easier than you might think to cook a whole meal on an outdoor grill without a kitchen nearby. Many of the recipes in this chapter can be cooked away from home—at a picnic area or on the beach. All it takes is a little advance preparation. You can put meats or fish in their marinade in the morning, pack them in a tightly covered container, and take them to the site in a picnic cooler. Even some hot foods (such as the rice to accompany the grilled shark on page 93) can be brought to the picnic at serving temperature in an insulated container. Just remember, for safety's sake, to keep hot foods hot and cold foods cold; without highly acid or highly salty marinades to protect them, perishable foods spoil quickly between 45° and 145°. Don't let them spend more than 4 hours (preferably much less time) between these two temperatures.

Lamb Satay with Peanut Sauce

In many of the world's languages, paired consonants are rare and therefore difficult to pronounce. When cooks in what is now Malaysia prepared what their British colonial masters called *steak*, it came out *satay* (sometimes spelled *saté*). The way they cooked it has become popular throughout Southeast Asia. The meat is thinly sliced, strung on skewers, grilled, and usually served with a creamy, spicy peanut sauce. The peanut sauce in this recipe is traditional, but the marinade is not. Paula Hogan, who helped me develop and test the recipes in this book, suggested the orange juice; I think it's a delicious touch.

Serves 2 as a main dish, 4 as an appetizer or with other dishes

½ pound (after trimming) boneless lamb leg or sirloin

Marinade
3 tablespoons orange juice
1½ teaspoons molasses
1 teaspoon oil
1 teaspoon soy sauce
1 small clove garlic, smashed
3 small slices ginger, smashed
¼ teaspoon salt
⅛ teaspoon pepper

Sauce
½ cup peanut butter
1 tablespoon lemon or lime juice
1 teaspoon soy sauce
1 tablespoon brown sugar
1 tablespoon peanut oil
1 heaping tablespoon minced shallot or onion
2 teaspoons minced ginger
1 teaspoon minced garlic
½ teaspoon ground coriander
¼ teaspoon red pepper flakes
½ cup water (approximately)

1. Separate the meat along the natural seams and trim each muscle to remove the fat and membranes. Slice the meat thinly across the grain into strips no more than 1 inch wide (the pieces will naturally come out different lengths; don't worry, just try to get the thickness the same). Combine the marinade ingredients in a bowl and toss the meat slices in the marinade. Let them stand 30 minutes to 2 hours.

2. For the sauce, put the peanut butter in a medium mixing bowl. Combine the lemon juice and soy sauce and stir in the brown sugar. Heat the oil in a skillet over medium heat and add all the remaining ingredients except the water. Cook until the shallot softens and the mixture is very fragrant. Scrape the contents of the skillet into the mixing bowl. Add the lemon juice mixture to the pan, heat it for a few seconds, and add it to the bowl. Stir to combine all the ingredients. Add the water to the pan, bring it to a boil, and add a little at a time to the sauce, stirring vigorously, until it is about the consistency of mayonnaise. Taste for seasoning and correct if necessary. (Most peanut butter supplies plenty of salt; if you use an unsalted variety, you will probably want to add salt.) Set the sauce aside at room temperature until you are ready to serve.

3. Drain the meat, reserving the marinade. Thread the meat on thin skewers, passing the skewer through each piece several times and stretching the meat out almost flat along the skewer. Combine smaller pieces as necessary to make skewers of nearly equal size. Grill the meat over a hot fire or broil it, basting occasionally with the marinade, until it is done to your taste, 2 to 3 minutes per side. Serve with the peanut sauce.

VARIATION Pork, beef, or dark meat turkey or chicken are equally delicious cooked this way.

NOTE This makes a rather pale peanut sauce. If you prefer a darker sauce and a toastier flavor, make your own peanut butter. Deep-fry raw peanuts until medium brown (see Sichuan Chile Peanuts, page 31, for technique) and grind them to peanut butter in a food processor.

Sandwiches To Go

Like any other food, a sandwich reflects the ingredients you put in it and the care with which you combine them. A ham and cheese sandwich on rye is only as good as the ham, the cheese, and the rye, so it's worth going to some trouble to find out which kinds of each you like best and how you like them put together. Here are five of my favorite sandwiches to go with beer. They'll taste just as good at home as on a grassy slope.

THE ULTIMATE HAM AND CHEESE SANDWICH Spread 2 slices of rye bread with about 1 teaspoon of Dijon or other strong mustard. Add 3 ounces of sliced (not too thin) Black Forest-style ham and 1 ounce of sliced Edam or Leiden cheese.

TURKEY SANDWICH #1 Spread 1 slice of rye or whole wheat bread with 1 teaspoon of mayonnaise; add 3 to 4 ounces of sliced turkey. Top with 2 teaspoons of mango chutney (bottled or homemade; see page 74), chopping up any large pieces first. Add a layer of lettuce leaves and the other slice of bread. Variation: Try thinly sliced roast pork in place of turkey.

TURKEY SANDWICH #2 Combine a pinch of curry powder with the mayonnaise in the above sandwich and substitute 1 tablespoon of whole cranberry sauce for the chutney.

SALMONBURGERS Mash 1 tall can (15½ ounces) sockeye salmon, including the juices, with a fork. Mix in 1 egg and 2 tablespoons dry bread crumbs, and season to taste with salt and pepper. Form into 4 hamburger-sized patties. Cut a large onion into coarse dice and cook over medium heat in 2 to 3 tablespoons butter until lightly browned. Lay the salmon patties on top of the onions and cook until both are well browned, 4 to 5 minutes per side. Serve hot or cold on onion rolls, spread with mayonnaise seasoned to taste with horseradish and chopped parsley.

CALAMARI VINAIGRETTE SANDWICH Clean 1 pound squid (see page 28), cut the mantles open lengthwise, and cut them into thin strips. Boil in lightly salted water just until opaque (about 30 seconds), drain, and rinse with cold water. Make a vinaigrette with 2 teaspoons vinegar, ¼ teaspoon salt, a large pinch of pepper, 2 tablespoons olive oil, and hot pepper sauce to taste. Toss the squid in the dressing and add ½ cup thinly sliced vegetables such as celery, sweet peppers, and sweet onions, and a teaspoon of capers. Let stand a few hours to overnight in the refrigerator. Remove some of the soft center of 4 long sandwich rolls, line with tender lettuce leaves, and fill with the squid mixture. Wrap tightly and serve within a few hours.

Garlic Prawns Grilled in Foil

Meat, fish, or poultry grilled over a charcoal fire that is still getting started can have an unpleasant, tar-like smoke flavor. But the fire seems to take forever to reach the perfect cooking stage when you have hungry guests standing around. Here's a solution: Cook an appetizer wrapped in foil so the smoke never touches the food. This recipe is an adaptation of Chinese Salt and Pepper Prawns, normally cooked in a wok. It will keep everyone happy until the main dish is cooked.

Serves 4 to 6 as an appetizer, 2 to 3 as a main dish

> ¾ *pound medium (31 to 40 per pound) or large (26 to 30 per pound) shrimp in the shell*
> 1 *tablespoon oil*
> 1 *tablespoon each minced ginger and garlic*
> 2 *tablespoons minced green onion*
> ½ *teaspoon kosher salt*
> ½ *teaspoon black pepper*
> *Lemon or lime wedges*

1. With small scissors, or with a paring knife cutting *outward*, slit each shrimp shell along the outer curve to expose the "vein" underneath. Remove the vein and rinse and drain the shrimp well.

2. In a bowl, combine the shrimp with the oil and seasonings and toss to coat them evenly. Spread about a dozen shrimp in a single layer on a sheet of heavy-duty aluminum foil; fold it into a neat package, sealing the edges well. Repeat with the remaining shrimp. Place the packets seam side up on the grill over a hot charcoal fire and cook until the packets puff up and the shrimp feel springy through the foil when pressed, 6 to 8 minutes for medium shrimp, 8 to 10 minutes for large. Unwrap and serve immediately, to peel and eat with the fingers. Set out a small bowl of lemon wedges for seasoning the shrimp to taste.

VARIATION If you don't want to deal with the shrimp shells, peel and devein the shrimp and cut the amount of salt and pepper in half. Reduce the cooking time by about a third.

Barbecued Ribs with Plum Sauce

I have always liked barbecue sauces based on fruit rather than tomatoes, and yet I almost never buy fruit to make a sauce. All my best batches have been opportunistic, made with fruit from the back yard trees and bushes wherever I was living at the time—a couple of scrawny volunteer plum trees here, a loquat tree there, a tangle of blackberry vines in another place. Use more or less vinegar and sugar according to the flavor of the fruit and you can make a good sauce from almost any cooked and pureed fruit. This shortcut version is based on store-bought jam.

Serves 3 to 4

Sauce
1 cup plum preserves
¼ cup cider vinegar
2 tablespoons minced ginger
2 cloves garlic, minced
1 medium onion, grated
1 tablespoon pure California or New Mexico chile powder (see page 85)
½ teaspoon salt

✿

½ teaspoon kosher salt
¼ teaspoon paprika
⅛ teaspoon each black and white pepper
Large pinch cayenne, or to taste
1 slab pork spareribs

1. Combine all the sauce ingredients in a saucepan. Bring it to a boil, reduce the heat, and simmer until no raw onion flavor remains and the sauce is slightly thickened, about 35 minutes. Makes 1 cup.

2. Prepare a medium-hot charcoal fire off center in a covered grill. Place a drip pan under the grill on the other side. Combine the salt, paprika, peppers, and cayenne and rub the mixture all over the ribs. Start cooking the ribs directly over the fire; cook until the fat begins to drip onto the fire and flare up, about 5 minutes. Turn the ribs and move them to the other side of the grill, over the drip pan. Cover the grill, leaving the vents fully open. Cook 1 hour, turning and rotating the ribs every 15 minutes. Baste with a little of the barbecue sauce thinned with water or beer during the last 15 minutes; serve with additional sauce at the table.

VARIATION Tightly sealed in a jar in the refrigerator, leftover sauce will keep for several weeks. Try it on barbecued chicken or other cuts of pork, such as country-style spareribs.

Grilled Shark with Assorted Salsas

Nothing brings out the flavor of a good piece of fish better than plain grilling, preferably over a charcoal fire. A simple Mexican-style tomato salsa is a perfect accompaniment, but you don't have to use tomatoes, especially when they are out of season. In winter, for example, try a version based on papaya and grapefruit.

Although this recipe calls for shark, you can use steaks of any similarly meaty fish, including swordfish, tuna, albacore, and halibut, or filets of smaller fish such as bass, red snapper, lingcod, tilefish, or rockfish.

Serves 4

> *4 shark steaks, about ¾ inch thick (5 to 7 ounces each)*
> *Pinch of salt and pepper*
> *1 tablespoon each olive oil and lemon or lime juice*
> *Cooked rice*

1. One to 2 hours ahead of serving time, prepare one or more of the salsas. Start a hot charcoal fire and clean and preheat the grill thoroughly. When the fire is getting going, place the shark steaks in a shallow dish, season them lightly with salt and pepper, and sprinkle them with the oil and lemon juice.

2. When the fire has reached the glowing red stage, grill the fish until done by the skewer test (see page 97), about 4 minutes per side. Serve with rice; spoon the salsa on top of the fish.

VARIATION   If you want more of a platform for the salsa, cut the steaks in half horizontally, making two thin steaks per serving instead of one thick one. Pay extra attention to the fish as it cooks, as thinner pieces can dry out with just a few seconds' overcooking.

NOTES   If cooking at a picnic site, you can cook the rice ahead of time and bring it to the picnic in an insulated container that will keep it warm. Or wrap the rice in a packet of heavy-duty foil and reheat it on the grill. Or forget about the rice and warm a batch of corn or flour tortillas on the grill just before cooking the fish.

If the shark is less than perfectly fresh or shows any trace of ammonia odor, soak it in mildly acidulated water (1 tablespoon vinegar or lemon juice to 2 cups water) for 30 minutes before marinating.

A Salsa Sampler

For each of the following salsas, simply combine all the ingredients in a bowl, let it stand for at least half an hour for the flavors to blend, and taste for seasoning before serving. Makes 1 cup.

PAPAYA-GRAPEFRUIT SALSA ½ cup each peeled grapefruit sections and finely diced papaya; 1 small green or red chile, seeds and ribs removed, minced; salt, to taste; cilantro or mint leaves, for garnish.

MEXICAN SALSA CRUDA 1 cup peeled, seeded, and chopped tomato; 1 small green chile, seeds and ribs removed, minced; 1 green onion, thinly sliced; 2 tablespoons chopped cilantro; salt, to taste.

THAI TOMATO SALSA 1 cup peeled, seeded, and chopped tomato; 1 small green chile, seeds and ribs removed, minced; 1 green onion, thinly sliced; 12 large mint or basil leaves, chopped; pinch of sugar; 1 teaspoon Thai fish sauce (see page 72).

Pistachio and Green Peppercorn Pâté

A good pâté served with thinly sliced bread, some fine mustard, and tiny pickles (*cornichons*) makes elegant picnic fare. This style of coarse-textured pâté, known in French as *pâté de campagne* (country style), is really no more difficult to make than a meat loaf. The only added step is cooling the pâté under a weight to give it a dense, even texture. If you have a French-style terrine (an oval or rectangular earthenware baking dish especially for this kind of thing), by all means use it. However, a pair of ordinary bread pans does the job nicely and produces an easy shape for uniform slices.

Makes about 2 pounds (serves 12 to 16 as an appetizer)

½ pound caul fat
1 pound ground veal
1 pound ground pork
½ cup finely diced onion
2 large eggs
¼ cup roasted shelled pistachios, roughly chopped
1 tablespoon canned green peppercorns, drained and chopped
1 teaspoon kosher salt
½ teaspoon mixed dried herbs (see Note)
Large pinch ground cloves
2 tablespoons Cognac or Armagnac

BEER NOTE This deserves a fine Pilsner or international-style lager, preferably in an elegant tall Pilsner glass. An India Pale Ale is another good choice.

1. Preheat the oven to 350°. Line the bottom and sides of a 9- by 4-inch loaf pan (the "terrine") with caul fat, draping enough over the sides to enclose the top.

2. Combine all the remaining ingredients in a large bowl and knead with your hands to blend thoroughly. Saute or boil a small sample of the mixture and taste it for seasoning; correct if necessary. Pack the mixture firmly into the terrine and bring the caul fat up over the top. Seal the top well with heavy-duty foil and place the terrine in a roasting pan. Place the roasting pan on a lower oven shelf and pour in boiling water to at least a third of the height of the loaf pan. Bake the pâté to an internal temperature of 160°, about 1 hour and 45 minutes.

3. Lift the terrine out of the roasting pan. Dump out the water, set the pan on a cooling rack, and put the terrine back in. Loosen the foil and set another loaf pan on top of it. Weight the top pan with 2 or 3 one-pound cans or jars and let the pâté cool for an hour or two, then refrigerate it (still weighted) overnight.

4. Before serving, remove the fat and jellied meat juices from the top of the pâté. Serve slices directly from the terrine, or unmold the pâté by setting the terrine into a hot water bath until the fat around the edges begins to melt, then turn it out onto a platter. Store any leftover pâté tightly wrapped in the refrigerator for up to 10 days.

NOTES Caul fat is a thin, transparent membrane veined with fat from the outside of a pig's stomach. As the pâté is baked, most of the fat melts away along with the fat from the meat, leaving the pâté tidily wrapped in an edible and attractive package. Ask for caul fat at specialty butcher shops and store any excess in the freezer.

Various blends of dried herbs will work here; most include thyme, which provides a good basic flavor. I use an *herbes de Provence* blend of thyme, marjoram, basil, rosemary, and savory. Other blends, labeled *fines herbs* or *bouquet garni,* may include tarragon, parsley, or chervil.

Grilled White Sausages with Red Chard

Mild-tasting white sausages made of pork and veal (sometimes chicken) are popular throughout northern Europe. They go by various names, including *boudin blanc, weisswurst,* and *bockwurst.* These sausages are fully cooked and need just to be reheated for serving. Grilling or broiling them gives a beautiful brown color to the skins and adds a slightly caramelized flavor.

BEER NOTE Munich is famous for *weisswurst,* and an amber Munich-style lager is its traditional partner, but this dish will go with any good lager or Pale Ale.

Serves 4

1½ pounds white sausages
1 bunch red-stemmed chard
1 tablespoon oil
Pinch of salt

1. Prepare a medium-hot charcoal fire in an uncovered grill. Remove the sausages from the refrigerator or picnic cooler 15 minutes before grilling.

2. Slice the chard stems into ½-inch diagonal pieces. Slice the leaves into larger strips, about an inch wide.

3. Grill the sausages on one side until well browned, 3 to 5 minutes depending on the heat of your fire. Turn or roll them over and brown the other side. (Some of the skins may burst, but the flavor will not be

96

affected.) Meanwhile, heat the oil in a skillet and lightly sauté the chard just until heated through. (You can do this right on the grill, alongside the sausages if your fire is big enough, or after removing the sausages from the grill.) Sprinkle the chard with a little salt and serve it alongside the sausages. Fried potatoes are a nice garnish if you are at home.

Grilled Fish with Mustard Glaze

Seafood and beer make great partners, and so do mustard and beer. The three also make a delicious trio, as this dish demonstrates. This recipe works best with moderately rich, meaty fish such as bluefish, striped bass, sea trout, California white seabass, yellowtail and other jacks, and mahi-mahi. The mustard flavor is a bit too much with stronger, darker fish such as tuna and mackerel.

Serves 4

1 to 1½ pounds fish filet
Salt
2 tablespoons Dijon-style mustard
1 tablespoon olive oil
1 teaspoon chopped fresh herbs such as oregano, marjoram, or tarragon
Fresh herb leaves, for garnish

1. Season the fish lightly with salt. Combine the mustard, oil, and herbs and rub the mixture over both sides of the fish. Set aside 30 minutes to 2 hours in the refrigerator.

2. If desired, place the fish in a wire grilling basket. Spread any of the mustard mixture remaining in the bowl over the fish. Grill over a hot charcoal fire until a thin skewer easily penetrates the thickest part of the fish, 3 to 5 minutes per side depending on the type and thickness of the fish. Garnish with leaves or sprays of the same herb as in the marinade.

The Skewer Test for Fish

The "skewer test" is the best way to test the doneness of fish. Start by poking a thin skewer or toothpick into the raw fish; feel how the point has to cut through the muscle tissue. Pierce the fish a couple of times as it cooks. You will feel little resistance as you poke through the outermost cooked layer, then more resistance as you hit the raw center. When just a bit of the raw feeling remains in the center, stop cooking. The cooking will finish over the next minute or two as the heat already in the fish penetrates to the center.

Jerk Thighs
(Jamaican Barbecued Chicken)

A few years ago I ate in a little Jamaican restaurant in Washington, D.C. The marinade on an order of "jerk" chicken thighs was the hottest thing I had ever tasted, much hotter than my previous scale-toppers, Thai green curries and Indonesian sambals. It took two tall glasses of sweet ginger punch (the restaurant didn't serve beer) to soothe my scorched palate. An authentic jerk marinade calls for the smallish chile known as "Scotch bonnet pepper" in the Caribbean, which is either the same as or nearly identical to the *chile habanero* of Yucatán. It's just plain too hot for my taste, even with plenty of beer. So here's a tamer version, using more commonly available small chiles. Like other hot foods, it goes with a cold lager or mild ale with a bit of sweetness. Another good choice is a sweet Stout, a style of beer very popular in the islands.

4 small fresh green or red chiles
4 green onions, trimmed
2 tablespoons vinegar (wine or cider)
1 tablespoon oil
1 tablespoon ground allspice
1 teaspoon salt
½ teaspoon pepper
½ teaspoon cinnamon
⅛ teaspoon nutmeg
8 chicken thighs, or 3 to 4 pounds chicken parts of your choice

1. Split the chiles lengthwise; remove and reserve the white ribs and seeds. Combine the chiles with all the remaining ingredients except the chicken in a food processor or blender and blend to a paste. Taste the paste; if you want it hotter, blend in some of the chile ribs and seeds. Spread the paste on the chicken and let it marinate in the refrigerator 1 to 4 hours.

2. Remove the chicken from the refrigerator 30 minutes before cooking. Grill it over a medium-hot fire in a covered grill until the juices run clear from near the bone, about 20 minutes. Baste occasionally with the marinade remaining in the bowl.

VARIATION Jerk marinades are also traditional for pork, goat, and other meats, as well as fish.

Fast and Easy:
Cornish Hens on the Grill

For a beautiful and aromatic alternative to roasted or barbecued chicken, try roasting Cornish hens on a covered grill. Rinse the birds well inside and out and pat them dry. Stuff the cavity of each with a green onion, a thick slice of ginger bruised with the side of a knife blade, a star anise pod, and a strip of fresh or dried orange peel. (Both star anise and dried orange peel are available in Chinese groceries.) Close up the cavity with a toothpick and rub a teaspoon or two of dark Chinese soy sauce all over the skin. Build a hot fire off center in a covered grill, with a drip pan under the grill on the opposite side. Place the birds skin side up on the grill over the drip pan, cover, and roast the hens to an internal temperature of 160°, about 30 minutes. Rotate the hens once during cooking, turning the side that was away from the heat toward it. (For normal-size frying chickens, use twice the ingredients for each bird and increase the cooking time to about 45 minutes.) Serve hot, lukewarm, or cold. For extra sheen and aroma, rub a little Asian sesame oil over the skin before serving. Serve with a fine Pilsner or other dry lager.

Nothing too bitter; try an English sweet Stout or Brown Ale.

Beer and Dessert

Only the most fanatical players of the beer and food matching game will want to plan a separate beer for the dessert course. But for those who want to continue sipping beer through dessert, some styles will clearly taste better than others. The main variable is sweetness, both in the beer and in the food. As with wine, trying to match the sweetness of the beer too closely to that of the food can be tricky; often a better approach is to look for contrast rather than consonance. You can go to one extreme by serving a dry Stout with dessert; dry, bitter, and astringent like a cup of strong black coffee, it serves as a foil to a rich, sweet chocolate dessert. But with a gentler, less sweet and less rich dessert like this one or the rice pudding on page 45, I would serve a sweeter English-style Stout, perhaps in the "Imperial" style. If you prefer something between these extremes, English Brown Ale is also sometimes recommended for dessert.

Elaine's Apple-Ginger Cake

My wife came up with this recipe for a seashore clambake. We needed something easy to transport and suitable for serving directly from the pan. It tastes just as good at home.

Serves 16

3 medium apples
6 tablespoons butter (room temperature)
1 cup sugar
2 tablespoons grated ginger
Zest of 1 lemon
2 tablespoons molasses
1 large egg
1¾ cups all-purpose flour
¼ teaspoon baking soda
½ teaspoon baking powder
2 teaspoons cinnamon
½ cup milk
1 cup walnuts, coarsely chopped

Ginger Icing
2 cups powdered sugar
2 teaspoons powdered ginger
3 tablespoons water

1. Preheat the oven to 375°. Butter and flour a 9-inch square cake pan. Peel and core the apples and cut them into 1-inch cubes. Set aside.

2. Cream the butter and sugar together until light. Add the ginger, lemon zest, and molasses and blend well. Add the egg and beat until smooth. Set aside ¼ cup of the flour. Sift the remaining flour with the baking soda, baking powder, and cinnamon. Add ⅓ of the flour mixture to the batter and mix well. Add ½ of the milk, another ⅓ of the flour, the rest of the milk, and the rest of the flour, mixing well after each addition. Toss the apple cubes in the reserved flour and stir them into the batter. Stir in the nuts. Transfer the batter to the prepared pan and bake until the cake springs back when lightly touched in the center, about 50 minutes. Cool in the pan on a wire rack.

3. When the cake is cool, sift together the powdered sugar and powdered ginger. Stir in 2 tablespoons of water. Stir in the remaining water a teaspoon at a time until the icing is smooth and easily spreadable (it may

take less water, or a little more). Spread the icing over the cake. To serve, cut the cake into squares and serve from the pan.

VARIATION   If you prefer, you can skip the icing and simply sift 2 tablespoons of powdered sugar over the cake.

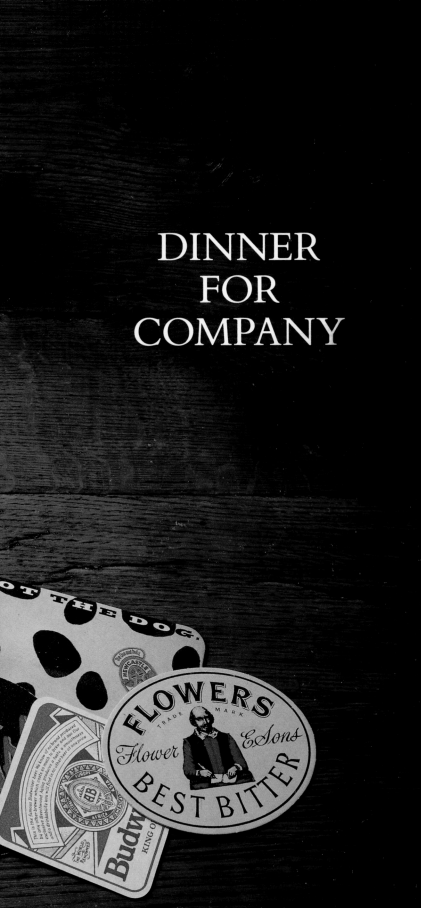

DINNER
FOR
COMPANY

**Pan-Fried Fish
with Malaysian Bean Sauce
Kung Pao Fish Filets
Braised Salmon with Cumin
Charcoal-Roasted Pork Loin
Braised Lamb Shanks with Olives
Bistec Criolla
Carbonnade Flamande
Rabbit Couscous with Apricots
Brazilian Chicken Baked
in Dark Beer
Duck Braised in Ale
Grilled Duck Breasts
with Sichuan Peppercorns**

Brazilian Chicken Baked in Dark Beer
(recipe, pg. 118)

Pan-Fried Fish with Malaysian Bean Sauce

This chile-spiked bean sauce is a popular topping for fried fish in Malaysia and Singapore. It's suitable for any lean, mild-tasting white fish, either pan-dressed whole fish or steaks or filets of larger fish. For cooking whole, try catfish, perch, smaller croakers, or various freshwater "panfish." Good choices among larger fish include sea bass, grouper, rockfish, lingcod, and larger croakers and drums.

Serves 2

> 2 whole pan-sized fish (about ½ pound each), cleaned and scaled, heads
> removed if desired **or** 1 pound thick fish steaks or filets
> Cornstarch
> Oil for frying
> ½ small onion or 2 shallots
> 2 cloves garlic
> 3 quarter-sized slices ginger
> 2 small fresh chiles (preferably red), seeds and ribs removed
> 2 tablespoons salted soybeans, drained and lightly mashed
> ¼ cup water
> Pinch of sugar
> Juice of ½ lime or lemon
> Cilantro sprigs for garnish

1. Rinse the fish well inside and out and pat them dry. Sprinkle heavily with cornstarch, rubbing it all over the fish inside and out.

2. Heat at least 1 inch of oil in a wok or large skillet. While the oil is heating, mince the onion, garlic, ginger, and chiles together finely. When the oil reaches 375°, slide the fish into it. (When the oil is hot enough a dry wooden chopstick inserted in it will emit a lively crown of bubbles.) Fry until the fish are crisp and golden on both sides, 3 to 4 minutes per side. Drain them on paper towels, then transfer them to a warm platter.

3. Let the oil cool slightly, then pour or ladle all but about 1 tablespoon into a clean saucepan to save for another use (see page 67). Return the wok to medium heat and add the onion mixture. Cook until quite fragrant then add the beans, water, and sugar. Cook until slightly reduced, stir in the lime juice, and pour the sauce over the fish. Garnish with sprigs of cilantro.

VARIATION This treatment is also suitable for a larger whole fish, up to 3 pounds. Use a good-sized wok, deeper oil at a slightly lower temperature

The Main Event

In a meal of several courses, entree time may be time to shift from a pale lager or other light beer to a fuller-bodied, darker, richer beer. This is the perfect place in the meal to highlight a special beer such as a fine handcrafted domestic, British, or Belgian ale; a special holiday brew; or one of the many European classics.

BEER NOTE Any good international-style lager is appropriate, including most Asian examples.

(about 360°), and repeatedly ladle hot oil over the part of the fish that sticks out of the oil. You might wish to prepare the sauce separately in another pan rather than try to ladle out a large amount of hot oil after frying the fish.

NOTE Salted and fermented yellow-tan soybeans are the Southeast Asian equivalent of Cantonese black beans. Look for them in jars from Singapore or Hong Kong in well-stocked Chinese markets; they will be labeled "salted soya bean" or something similar. If you can't find them, use Chinese fermented black beans; rinse well to remove as much color as possible.

Kung Pao Fish Filets

Kung pao (or *gong bao*) dishes get their distinctive flavor from chiles cooked to the point of charring. The fumes can be a bit hard on the cook's nose, but the chiles give an incomparable flavor to the dish. *Kung pao* is usually a stir-frying technique, but I also like to use it as the base for a sauce for sauteed fish filets.

Serves 4

¼ cup chicken stock
1 tablespoon soy sauce
¼ teaspoon sugar
2 cloves garlic, minced
1 teaspoon minced ginger
White parts of 2 green onions, minced
2 tablespoons peanut or other vegetable oil
4 to 6 small dried chiles
1 to 1½ pounds mild white fish filets
¼ teaspoon salt (approximately)
¼ cup cornstarch (approximately)
½ cup sliced bamboo shoots, drained and cut into julienne pieces
½ cup julienned red bell pepper
¼ cup julienned green onion tops
1 tablespoon roasted peanuts, chopped

1. Combine the stock, soy sauce, and sugar and set aside. Combine the minced ingredients in a small bowl and set aside. If you have an exhaust fan in your kitchen, turn it to the maximum setting. Combine the oil and chiles in a large skillet and place it over medium-high heat until the

chiles are nearly black. Meanwhile, season the fish lightly with salt and dust it with cornstarch, shaking off the excess.

2. When the chiles are nearly black, discard them, reduce the heat to medium, and add the fish to the pan, bone side down (see Note). Cook until golden brown, turn, and continue cooking until a skewer easily enters the thickest part of the fish (see The Skewer Test, page 97). Total cooking time is 7 to 10 minutes per inch of thickness, depending on the type of fish. Transfer the fish to a warm platter.

3. Turn the heat under the skillet to medium-high. Add the minced ginger, garlic, and green onion and cook until fragrant, about 10 seconds. Add the bamboo shoots and peppers and cook, stirring, until the vegetables are heated through. Stir the liquid mixture to dissolve the sugar, add it to the pan along with the green onion tops, and bring it to a boil. Reduce the liquid by half, taste it for seasoning, and pour it over the fish. Garnish with chopped peanuts.

NOTE Even when you are dealing with skinless, boneless filets, it's usually easy to tell the skin side from the bone side. The skin side is generally smoother, with a pattern of lighter and darker colors clearly showing the layers of muscle in the meat. The side that was against the bones comes out a little bumpier, and may show the impressions left by the backbone and the ribs. I find the irregularities of the bone side more interesting to look at, so I always start with that side down in the pan; after turning once, it winds up on top, and goes onto the plate that way.

Light Beer with Fish, Dark Beer with Meat?

Is there a beer equivalent to the "white wine with fish, red wine with meat" rule? Not necessarily. In general, rich meats call for more flavorful and highly hopped beers, and those tend to be darker. But a dark dry Stout or Porter is also delicious with many seafood dishes, from plain oysters to fish filets in a creamy sauce. Conversely, I have thoroughly enjoyed drinking Pilsner with a rich spinach and cheese lasagna, a dish with which I would always choose red wine over white. Poultry can go either way, depending in large part on the sauce or other seasonings; chicken with a peppery barbecue sauce or marinade calls for a lighter, slightly sweet beer, while roast duck needs an assertive, hoppy ale. Overall, the flavor of the beer—sweet or dry, mild or highly hopped, light and crisp or rich and malty—is a better determining factor in how it will match with foods than its color.

Braised Salmon with Cumin

Braising, cooking in a covered pan with a small amount of liquid, is an ideal technique for firm, flavorful fish such as salmon. The cooking time in this recipe is based on ¾-inch steaks or slices; allow more cooking time for thicker steaks, a little less for thinner pieces.

Serves 2

> *1 tablespoon olive oil*
> *1 cup thinly sliced onion*
> *½ teaspoon cumin seeds*
> *1 tablespoon dry white wine, stock, or water*
> *2 salmon steaks or thick crosscut filets (6 to 7 ounces each)*
> *¼ teaspoon salt (approximately)*
> *Freshly ground pepper*
> *¾ to 1 teaspoon sherry vinegar*

Spring Seafood Menu

Beer-Steamed Clams or Mussels
Pilsner Urquell
Braised Salmon with Cumin
Fresh Asparagus
EKU Edelbock
Strawberry Shortcake

1. Choose a heavy skillet with a tight-fitting lid, preferably one just large enough to hold the salmon steaks rather snugly. Heat the skillet over low heat and add the oil and onion. Cook until the onion begins to wilt, about 2 minutes, then add the cumin seeds. Cover and cook slowly until the onion juices are nearly gone and the onion begins to brown, 10 to 12 minutes.

2. Push the onion to the sides of the pan. Add the liquid and bring it to a simmer. Season the salmon steaks with salt and pepper and lay them in the pan. Cover and cook, turning once, until a skewer easily penetrates the thickest part of the fish, 4 to 5 minutes per side (see The Skewer Test, page 97).

3. Transfer the cooked steaks to warm plates. Add ¾ teaspoon of vinegar to the skillet, turn the heat to high, and cook until the liquid is reduced to about a tablespoon. Taste for seasoning and add more salt, pepper, or vinegar if necessary. Spoon the onion mixture over and around the steaks.

VARIATION Try this treatment with Alaska halibut, king mackerel, mahi-mahi, or other fine-textured but firm fish.

Choosing a Roast

A roast can come from any part of the pork loin. The meat at the shoulder or blade end is less tender, but its higher fat content gives it more flavor. The sirloin end is the leanest and tenderest part, but the bone structure gets a little complicated. Center-cut roasts have the simplest bone structure and one large rib eye muscle, plus a nice compromise between flavor and tenderness; naturally, they command the highest price.

Charcoal-Roasted Pork Loin

A charcoal fire, a simple spice rub, and the malty aromas from the beer-based marinade under the meat combine to make a memorable pork roast that goes with just about any beer.

Serves 4 to 6

> 1 bone-in pork loin roast (about 3 pounds)
> 1 teaspoon kosher salt
> ½ teaspoon paprika
> ¼ teaspoon each black and white pepper
> ⅛ teaspoon cayenne, or more or less to taste
> ½ cup Stout or Porter

1. If the roast has been deeply cut (see Note), tie it at intervals to keep the chops together. Combine the salt with all the peppers and rub the mixture all over the outside of the meat. Place it in a bowl, add the Stout, and marinate 1½ to 8 hours, turning occasionally.

2. Build a medium-hot charcoal fire on one side of a covered grill, with a disposable foil pie pan under the grill on the opposite side. When the coals have reached the glowing red stage, pour half of the marinade into the pie pan, put the grill in place, and position the roast over the pan. Reserve the remaining marinade. Adjust the top and bottom vents so the fire maintains a temperature of 300 to 325° (an oven thermometer is a great help here). Cook, turning the roast every half hour or so, until the meat reaches an internal temperature of 160°, about 2½ hours. Add marinade to the drip pan if it appears to be drying out. Let the roast rest at least 15 minutes before carving.

NOTE For easier carving of a pork loin roast, have the butcher cut through the backbone at intervals with a band saw. If your roast comes from the forward rib section of the loin, it's a simple matter to cut through the backbone between the ribs. As you go farther back on the loin, the ribs are replaced by the T-bone familiar to beef lovers, and it takes a deeper cut with the saw to get through all the bone. In either case, carving is a simple matter of continuing the cut through to the other side, making thick chops.

Braised Lamb Shanks with Olives

This is a dish that is wonderful served with beer but would not benefit from being cooked in beer. Instead a full-flavored red wine provides acidity and a fruity flavor to balance the richness of the meat and the intense saltiness of the olives. All it needs is a good hoppy ale alongside and something like bread or potatoes to soak up the savory sauce.

Serves 2 to 3

1½ tablespoons olive oil
2 lamb shanks (1 to 1⅓ pounds)
Pepper, to taste
1 medium onion, diced (about 1 cup)
12 small whole garlic cloves
½ cup each finely diced carrot and celery
1 cup Zinfandel or other red wine
1 sprig of thyme
1 bay leaf
½ cup Kalamata or other black olives, pitted if possible

1. Heat the oil in a heavy flameproof casserole. Season the lamb shanks with pepper and brown them well on all sides. Remove and set them aside. Add the onion, garlic, carrot, and celery to the casserole and cook over medium heat until they are lightly browned. Return the lamb shanks to the casserole, add the wine, herbs, and olives, cover, and cook at a gentle simmer until the lamb is quite tender, about 2 hours.

2. Remove the lamb and vegetables to a serving dish with a slotted spoon. Discard the herbs. Place the pot off center over medium-high heat and bring the sauce to a boil. Skim off the fat that collects on the other side of the pot. When the sauce is sufficiently skimmed, taste it for seasoning and correct if necessary. Pour the sauce over the lamb and serve it with squares of cooked polenta (see page 120), mashed potatoes, or Beer Biscuits (see page 54).

"For a quart of ale is a dish for a king."
—William Shakespeare
The Winter's Tale

111

Bistec Criolla
(Steak with Diced Vegetable Relish)

This recipe was inspired by a dish cooked by Hubert Keller, executive chef of the Fleur de Lys restaurant in San Francisco. According to Chef Keller, who worked for a couple of years in Brazil prior to coming here, this sort of diced vegetable relish is widely used in South America to accompany grilled meats. The name, Spanish for *Creole,* is pronounced *creoja* in the dialect typical of Argentina and Chile.

I've purposely left the amount of beef vague here; use as much or as little as your appetite dictates. Personally, I don't eat steak anywhere near as often as I used to, and in any case I can't put away a big hunk of beef the way I could when I was in my twenties. I can now dine happily on half a restaurant-size steak, especially when it is sliced and fanned out on a plate.

Serves 4

Salsa Criolla
2 teaspoons wine vinegar
½ teaspoon kosher salt
⅛ teaspoon freshly ground black pepper
2 tablespoons olive oil
1 small red or yellow bell pepper
1 small zucchini
1 stalk celery
1 small tomato, seeded
1 small carrot, peeled
½ medium cucumber, peeled and seeded
¼ small sweet onion (preferably red), peeled
1 tablespoon chopped parsley
Liquid hot pepper sauce, to taste

✿

2 tender beef steaks (New York strip or Porterhouse), about 1 inch thick
Salt and pepper

1. For the salsa, combine the vinegar, ¼ teaspoon salt, and the pepper in a medium bowl and stir until the salt dissolves. Stir in the oil. Cut all the vegetables into uniform fine dice, between ⅛- and ¼-inch cubes. Add them to the bowl; add the parsley, the remaining salt, and a few dashes of hot pepper sauce. Toss to combine evenly and set aside for up to 2 hours for the flavors to combine.

BEER NOTE The choice of beer depends in part on how hot you make your salsa. If it's on the mild side, I would match the beer mostly to the flavor of the beef and choose a good dryish Porter. If you go heavier on the pepper sauce, a somewhat sweeter pale or amber lager is in order.

2. Warm a serving platter and dinner plates in a low oven. Grill or broil the steaks until done to your liking; season them with salt and pepper part way through cooking. Set the cooked steaks aside on the platter, loosely covered with foil, for about 5 minutes, then transfer them to a carving board and carve them diagonally into thin slices. Arrange the slices on the warm platter and spoon any juices from the cutting board on top. Taste the salsa for seasoning and adjust it as necessary. Serve the salsa on the side, to spoon over each serving of sliced beef.

Carbonnade Flamande (Beef and Onions Braised in Beer)

This rich, wintry stew is one of the most famous dishes of Flemish cuisine, and it goes wonderfully with a Belgian Trappist ale such as Chimay. It's also delicious with a fruity ale in the British tradition. Although Stout is a good choice for the cooking beer, I find it a little too much to drink alongside. Like most stewed dishes, this one is good reheated.

Serves 6

> *4 tablespoons oil*
> *1 beef rump or similar roast (2 to 2½ pounds), trimmed and sliced ¼ inch thick*
> *Salt and pepper*
> *2 pounds onions (about 4 medium), thinly sliced*
> *2 tablespoons all-purpose flour*
> *2 cups beef stock or canned beef broth*
> *1 bottle dry Stout or Porter*
> *1 teaspoon brown sugar, if needed*
> *1 teaspoon red wine vinegar*
> *3 sprigs parsley*
> *1 bay leaf*
> *1 sprig fresh thyme or ¼ teaspoon dried thyme*

1. Preheat the oven to 325°. Heat 1 tablespoon of the oil in a large skillet over medium-high heat. Season the beef slices lightly with salt and pepper and cook as many at a time as will fit in a single layer until all are nicely browned, about 1 minute per side. Transfer the slices to a plate and set aside.

A Beer-Based Cuisine

If any country could be said to have a beer cuisine (as opposed to food which goes well with beer) it would be Belgium. The country must have as many types of beer as France has cheeses, and their role at the dinner table is taken as seriously as that of wine in France. Carbonnade Flamande is only the best known of many classic Belgian dishes which use one sort of beer or another as an ingredient. One cookbook lists "the 300 best recipes" for dishes made with beer. It might take a lifetime to get to know such a variety of beers and the foods to go with them—but I intend to try in the years I have left!

2. Reduce the heat to medium-low and add the remaining oil to the skillet. Add the onions and cook, stirring occasionally, until they are golden brown, about 5 minutes. Lift the onions out of the skillet with a slotted spoon, leaving behind as much of the oil as possible.

3. Return the skillet to medium-high heat, stir in the flour, and cook, stirring, until the resulting roux is a medium brown. Add the stock, beer, and any accumulated juices from the meat plate. Cook, stirring to break up any lumps, until the sauce is lightly thickened. Taste for salt and add more if necessary; add the vinegar and a little brown sugar, if you like, to balance the bitterness of the beer. (Sugar may be unnecessary with some sweeter beers.)

4. Spread half the onions in the bottom of a shallow covered baking dish. Arrange the beef slices in a layer on top. Tie the herbs into a bundle (*bouquet garni*) with clean string and place it on top of the meat. (If using dried thyme, just scatter it in the pan.) Spread the rest of the onions on top. Pour the sauce over the meat and onions, cover the baking dish, and bake until the meat is quite tender, 2 to 2½ hours. Let it stand until the fat rises to the surface, then discard the herb bouquet and skim off the fat. Serve with steamed new potatoes or wide noodles.

A Good Bird and a Good Beer

One of the best dishes to serve when trying a new or special brew is a simple roast chicken. Here is my favorite cooking method: Remove the excess fat from a 3- to 4-pound frying chicken, rinse the bird well inside and out, and pat it dry. Combine ½ teaspoon kosher salt, ¼ teaspoon *each* freshly ground black pepper and paprika, ¼ teaspoon crumbled dried thyme, and a pinch of cayenne. Rub the mixture all over the chicken inside and out. Place it breast side up on a rack in a roasting pan and roast it in a preheated 350° oven until a thermometer inserted into the thigh registers 155°, about 18 minutes per pound. That's it—no trussing, no basting, no turning over.

For a delicious (though caloric) garnish, cut new potatoes into wedges and arrange them around the roasting rack to cook along with the chicken, absorbing the juices. Halfway through cooking, add 1 head of garlic, broken apart into unpeeled cloves. At the table squeeze the cooked garlic out of its skin onto the potatoes for an incomparable taste.

Rabbit Couscous with Apricots

One of my favorite chicken dishes in the world is the Chicken with Prunes, Rif Style in Paula Wolfert's *Couscous and Other Good Foods from Morocco*. Although this dish substitutes rabbit for the chicken, apricots for the prunes, and a simpler blend of spices, it is clearly derived from that traditional Moroccan dish. (It also works fine with skinned chicken.)

Serves 4

   1 frying rabbit (2½ to 3 pounds)
   ½ teaspoon cinnamon
   ½ teaspoon **garam masala** *(see page 69)*
   ¼ teaspoon salt
   ⅛ teaspoon pepper
   1 large onion, split vertically and thinly sliced
   2 cloves garlic, minced
   ¼ cup water
   1 to 2 tablespoons oil
   ½ cup dried apricot halves
   ⅔ cup dry white wine
   ½ cup beef stock or brown poultry or rabbit stock
   1½ cups couscous, cooked according to package directions

1. Disjoint the rabbit by cutting the hind and forelegs away from the back. Set aside the liver and kidneys, if present. Separate the center section of the back (the loin or saddle) from the rest of the back and cut it crosswise into 4 pieces. Use only the legs and loin; save the remaining parts of the carcass for stock.

2. Combine the cinnamon, garam masala, salt, and pepper. Rub half the mixture all over the rabbit pieces. Combine the onion and garlic with the remaining spice mixture and the water in a large flameproof casserole. Cover and cook over medium-low heat until the onions are soft, about 15 minutes.

3. Meanwhile, heat the oil in a skillet and brown the rabbit pieces well a few at a time. When the onions are soft, add the rabbit pieces and apricots to the casserole. Deglaze the skillet with the wine and add it to the casserole. Add the stock, cover, and simmer over low heat or cook in a 250° oven until the rabbit is quite tender, about 1 hour.

4. Spread the cooked couscous in a large serving dish, making a slight well in the center. Arrange the rabbit pieces on top and surround them with apricots and onions. Taste the sauce for seasoning, adjust it if necessary, and pour it over the rabbit. Serve with a crunchy, green vegetable.

BEER NOTE With the exuberant spicy, fruity flavors of this dish, this is no time for a pale, lightweight beer. Try a good dark lager or even a Doppelbock.

117

Brazilian Chicken Baked in Dark Beer (Galinha com Cerveja)

Dark beer and an array of herbs and peppers give a wonderfully deep, rich flavor to this dish from the Bahia region of Brazil. The long, moist baking makes the chicken especially tender. Both the flavor and the texture are even better the second day. The recipe is from São Paulo-born Valmor Neto, who serves it at his three Bahia Brazilian restaurants in San Francisco.

Serves 4

> *2 small frying chickens (about 2½ pounds each)*
> *1 small onion, sliced*
> *2 bottles (approximately) dark lager*
> *1 tablespoon chopped garlic*
> *2 teaspoons dried tarragon leaves*
> *2 teaspoons dried oregano leaves*
> *1½ teaspoons dried basil leaves*
> *2½ teaspoons paprika*
> *½ teaspoon black or white pepper*
> *½ teaspoon red pepper flakes*
> *1 tablespoon kosher salt*
> *1⅓ cups long-grain rice, cooked with ¼ teaspoon saffron threads*
> *Couve (left)*

1. Split the chickens in half and remove the backbones; split or remove the keel (breast) bone. Remove the second and third wing joints and any excess fat and flaps of skin. If you want a more compact shape, chop off the heel end of the drumstick with a cleaver. Arrange the chicken halves skin side down in a deep roasting pan or casserole and lay the onion slices on top. Add beer to nearly cover the chicken. Scatter the garlic, herbs, peppers, and salt over the surface and gently spoon the beer around to moisten everything evenly. Cover the pan with aluminum foil or a lid and marinate 2 hours to overnight in the refrigerator.

2. Preheat the oven to 400°. Remove the chicken from the refrigerator for about 30 minutes to let it come back to near room temperature. Bake the chicken, covered, for 1½ hours. Remove the foil or lid, turn the chicken halves skin side up, and return them to the oven to bake 15 minutes longer. Let them cool, then refrigerate overnight.

3. *On serving day:* Remove the excess fat from the surface of the sauce. Reheat the chicken and sauce uncovered in a 400° oven; if your baking

COUVE This traditional vegetable accompaniment to Bahian dishes is nothing more than finely shredded and sauteed collard greens. Remove the stems and thick central ribs from 1 large bunch of collards, roll up the leaves into manageable bundles, and slice them crosswise into fine shreds. Saute in a large skillet just until tender with 2 to 3 tablespoons of olive oil, a tablespoon of chopped garlic, and salt and pepper to taste.

dish is flameproof, you can reheat the chicken on top of the stove. When it is thoroughly reheated, lift the pieces out of the sauce and arrange them on a platter or individual plates; set aside and keep warm. Bring the sauce to a boil (transfer it to a large skillet first if your baking dish is not flameproof) and reduce the volume by about two-thirds, making a thick glaze. Spoon the glaze over the chicken and serve with saffron rice and sauteed *couve*.

NOTES If you want to serve the chicken on the same day you bake it, cook it a bit longer in step 2. Time the dish to come out of the oven about 10 minutes before serving time, then reduce the sauce as directed in step 3.

This recipe makes restaurant-size portions, with half a small chicken per person. If you have trouble finding fryers under 3 pounds, or if your appetite and baking dish are a little smaller, one large fryer (about 4 pounds) would suffice for 4 family-style servings. Two split Cornish hens would make 4 modest proportions, each containing both light and dark meat. With larger or smaller birds, you will need to adjust the initial (covered) cooking time.

BEER NOTE For both cooking and drinking with this dish, choose a rich, dark lager that is not too bitter. Xingu, the "black beer of the Amazon," is a fine choice for drinking, though Valmor Neto finds it a bit too strong to use by itself in the cooking. Instead, he mixes one part Xingu with two parts domestic dark lager.

Cutting Up a Duck

There is not a whole lot of meat on a duck, so it pays to go to some trouble to get it all. When cutting the legs from a whole duck, be sure to include as much meat as possible from around the hip joint. When removing the wings, remove the long shoulder blade bones along with them; scrape the attached meat toward the wing and remove the shoulder blade. Save the rest of the carcass for the stockpot.

Duck Braised in Ale

Duck breast lends itself to quick cooking on the grill (see page 122), but slower, moister cooking brings out the best in the leg and wing meat. For a little bit more than the price of the boneless breasts in the following recipe, you can get two whole ducks and cut them up yourself, and enjoy this delicious, tender duck stew as a bonus. (Some poultry markets that sell fresh ducks also sell the hindquarters separately.) Use a full-flavored Pale Ale that is not too bitter; Bass Ale from England is ideal.

Serves 4

> *Kosher salt*
> *Legs and wings of 2 ducks*
> *3 small onions, quartered*
> *1 bottle Pale Ale*
> *Freshly ground black pepper, to taste*
> *1 tablespoon olive oil or butter*
> *2 cups celery, in thick diagonal slices*
> *½ cup poultry or meat stock*
> *Pinch of salt*
> *Polenta triangles (see Note)*

1. Heat a wok or large cast-iron skillet over high heat and sprinkle it generously with salt. Sear the duck pieces a few at a time, cooking mainly on the skin side and adjusting the heat so the fat does not smoke. Cook, turning occasionally, until the skin is well browned and has rendered some of its fat. As the duck pieces are done, transfer them to a flameproof covered casserole. Discard the fat in the wok.

2. Scatter the onions over the duck in the casserole and add the ale and a few grindings of pepper. Bring to a boil, cover, and cook at a simmer or in a 250° oven until the duck is quite tender, about 1¼ hours.

3. When the duck is about 10 minutes away from done, heat the oil in a small skillet or saucepan and briefly saute the celery. Add the stock, cover, and stew 5 minutes. Remove from the heat and keep warm.

4. Transfer the duck pieces and onions to a serving dish, top with the celery, and keep warm. Use a gravy separator to remove the fat from the cooking liquid, or transfer it to a deep glass pitcher and siphon the liquid from under the fat with a bulb baster. Return the defatted liquid to the pan, bring it to a boil, and reduce it by a third. Pour this sauce over the duck and serve with triangles of polenta.

NOTE To make polenta triangles, cook polenta as described in Braised

Sausages with Polenta (page 77), then pour a ½-inch-thick layer into a lightly oiled rectangular baking pan. Let it stand until firm, about 30 minutes, or chill overnight. Cut the polenta into triangles (or sticks, or any other shape) and reheat it in a lightly oiled skillet or a hot oven.

Grilled Duck Breasts with Sichuan Peppercorns

Dry-marinating in a salt and spice mixture and long, slow steaming are traditional Chinese techniques for ridding duck of its excess fat. A final grilling over a very hot fire imparts a crisp texture and smoky flavor. In this dish curly endive adds a refreshing and balancing note of bitterness; try it with a full-flavored Danish or German lager, or the Chinese Tsingtao.

Serves 4

1½ teaspoons Sichuan peppercorns (see Sichuan Chile Peanuts, page 31)
1 tablespoon kosher salt
4 boned duck breast halves, with skin attached
1 small head curly endive
1 tablespoon red wine vinegar
Freshly ground black pepper

1. Toast the Sichuan peppercorns in a skillet until quite fragrant. Crush them in a mortar or grind them in a spice grinder and combine them with the salt. Rub the mixture all over the duck breasts, a little heavier on the skin side. Place them in a shallow bowl, cover, and refrigerate 4 hours to overnight.

2. Drain the duck breasts and arrange them skin side up in a shallow heat-proof dish that will fit on a rack inside a wok. (A glass pie pan is ideal.) Fit the steaming rack in the wok, add water to an inch below the rack, and bring it to a boil. Place the dish on the rack, cover, and steam 45 minutes. Every 10 minutes or so, remove the cover and draw out the accumulated duck juices with a bulb baster; reserve them. Add boiling water to the wok if necessary to keep it from boiling dry.

3. If time permits, lay the duck breasts skin side up on a cooling rack in a drafty place for 1 to 2 hours to dry the skin. Let the duck juices stand until the fat separates, then skim off and discard the fat.

4. Build a hot fire in a covered grill. While the coals are getting ready, tear the endive into small pieces, discarding the heavy stems and darkest outer leaves. Wash and spin it dry; set it aside in a heatproof bowl.

5. Grill the breasts skin side down until well browned and crisp, about 8 minutes. Meanwhile, combine ¼ cup of the defatted duck drippings with the vinegar and pepper in a skillet and warm it slightly. Pour this dressing over the endive, toss to coat it evenly, then arrange it on plates or a serving platter. Slice the duck breasts crosswise, with a bit of skin attached to each slice, and arrange them on top of the greens.

TECHNIQUE NOTE It's possible to prepare this dish from start to finish in an afternoon, but it is much more convenient to spread the work out over a couple of days. Marinate the duck breasts one day, steam them the next, and you can keep them in the refrigerator for up to three days after that before the final grilling. Remove them from the refrigerator an hour before the final cooking.

Bibliography

Casas, Penelope. *Tapas: The Little Dishes of Spain.* New York: Knopf, 1985.

_____. *The Foods and Wines of Spain.* New York: Knopf, 1982.

Eckhardt, Fred. *The Essentials of Beer Style.* Portland, OR: All Brewers Information Service, 1989.

Goldstein, Joyce. *The Mediterranean Kitchen.* New York: William Morrow and Company, 1989.

Jackson, Michael. *The New World Guide to Beer.* Philadelphia: Running Press, 1988.

_____. *The Simon & Schuster Pocket Guide to Beer.* New York: Simon & Schuster, 1988.

McGee, Harold. *On Food and Cooking: The Science and Lore of the Kitchen.* New York: Scribner's 1984.

Rosengarten, David. "The Case for Beer." *Food & Wine,* August 1990.

Appendix

The Brewing Process

The broadest definition of *beer* covers a variety of fermented beverages made from grains. But as it is used in this book, beer (including ale, see page 10) is a beverage of low alcoholic strength made from water and barley malt, and sometimes other grain products, and flavored with hops.

Unlike wine, beer is entirely a "made" product. A winemaker must work with the year's crop of grapes, and can only vary the final wine within a certain range. A cold summer or early rains can mean underripe or watery grapes, and the resulting wine will be different from one made in a year of abundant sunshine. It is these differences from year to year that make "vintage" such an important word in the world of wine.

On the other hand, barring a catastrophic failure of the grain or hop harvest or a change in the local water supply, a brewer can make the same type of beer year in and year out simply by following the same recipe. The closest thing to grape vintages the brewer faces is subtle variation from year to year in the flavor of the hops; but it's a simple matter to adjust the amount to compensate for more or less aroma or bitterness.

In fact, it is this consistency of style that is the hallmark of the world's great brews. Some brewers intentionally create seasonal brews, varying the recipe from year to year and bottling them with "vintage years"; but by and large, when a brewery has a successful formula they stick with it.*

Brewing is both an art and a science. The art of the brewer is to manipulate a number of very complex chemical reactions to produce the sometimes subtle differences between one type of beer and another. The steps of the process by which water, grain, hops, and yeast become beer are out-

lined in simplified form below. The variables at each step—the type and amount of malt used, the type of yeast, the varieties and amounts of hops used and the timing of their use, and the temperature of fermentation and aging—all work together to determine if the beer will be a pale, dry, refreshing Pilsner; a rich, sweetish amber Bock beer; a fruity, hoppy Pale Ale; an espresso-colored Stout; or any of a number of other styles.

MALTING   To turn dry, stable grain into fermentable form, the whole grain is moistened and allowed to germinate. Enzymes within the grain convert the starchy center into an assortment of sugars, most of which are fermentable by yeast. The length of time and the temperature of the malting step determine how much of the grain is converted to fermentable sugars and how much remains as unfermentable carbohydrates, or dextrins. A higher proportion of dextrins will result in a sweeter and "maltier" beer; fewer dextrins make for a drier, "cleaner" taste.

When the desired amount of conversion has taken place, the maltster kilns (roasts) the grain, drying it to stop the enzyme action and adding some roasted color and flavor. A light roasting yields a pale golden extract familiar to lager drinkers; a medium or Vienna roast produces an amber brew with a more assertive flavor; and darker roasts range from medium brown to almost black, with flavor overtones of chocolate, coffee, or burnt caramel. The malted grain is now ready for brewing, or for many months of storage; unlike winemakers, who are tied to the annual grape harvest, brewers can begin a new batch of beer any time they please.

MASHING   After roasting, the malt is crushed or ground, then soaked in warm water for several hours to dissolve the sugars and a small amount of protein and reactivate the enzymes. The liquid, now called wort, is filtered to remove the grain husks and other solids, then boiled with hops. Boiling destroys any remaining enzymes as well as wild yeasts or other organisms that might spoil the brew, and extracts the bitter flavor from the hops.

The aromatic dried blossoms of a tall-growing vine, hops are only one of the herbal substances that have been

---

*Although formulas for even the most successful beers do change with time; beer historian Fred Eckhardt notes that the amount of hop flavor in Budweiser declined by 30 percent from 1981 to 1987.

used throughout history to flavor and preserve beer. Juniper berries, spruce shoots, and various herbs can be used in similar ways, but the hop has proven the most reliable of all. A distinctive, complex mixture of essential oils, acids, and tannins in hops provides flavor, aroma, and some natural preservatives to the beer. Unfortunately, most of the desirable volatile aromas are driven off when the wort is boiled, so additional hops (often a second variety) are added at the end to contribute their aroma as well as flavor to the wort.

Like grapes, apples, and other crops, hops come in many varieties, and the same variety can produce different flavors and aromas according to where it is grown. Some offer more bitterness, others are used for their particular aroma. Not surprisingly, most of the world's famous hop varieties are identified with the major brewing regions of Europe: Saaz from Bohemia, Hallertau and others from Bavaria, Fuggles and Goldings from the English county of Kent are among the most famous. It is fitting that the Pacific Northwest has become a hotbed of new brewing activity, as the hop harvest in the interior part of the region (mostly Washington State east of the Cascades, which give their name to an important variety) makes the U.S. second only to Germany in worldwide hop production.

FERMENTATION After another straining and rapid cooling, the wort is ready for fermentation. The brewer introduces a cultivated strain of yeast, a single-celled fungus which can feed on the dissolved sugars. The yeast cells rapidly multiply in the wort, and in a few days to a couple of weeks they convert most of the sugars to ethyl alcohol and carbon dioxide. For now, the carbon dioxide is allowed to escape or, in large breweries, is collected for another use.

The alcoholic strength of beer is basically a function of the amount of dissolved sugars in the wort, and is usually determined by the style the brewer is trying to attain. Beers intended for daily refreshment, including the draft beers consumed every day by European workers as well as summertime specialties such as Berliner Weisse, are intentionally at the lower end of the spectrum, approximately 2.5 to 4 percent alcohol by volume. Darker, richer seasonal specialties such as Bock or Märzen beer, as well as most ales, are usually somewhat stronger at 4 to 6 percent; these fuller-flavored brews need a little more strength to provide a balanced flavor. "Strong" ales, "double" Bocks, Imperial Stouts, and barley wines, at up to 8 percent alcohol, are near the limit of strength that beer yeasts can survive, which is still lower than the 11 to 14 percent alcohol of table wines. These are not everyday brews, but special beers meant to be sipped in smaller quantities.

The type of yeast and the fermenting temperature determine whether the final product is an ale or a lager. For ales, the older of the two styles, the fermentation occurs at cellar or room temperature (58 to 68°) and the yeast forms a thick mat near the top of the liquid. These "top-fermenting" yeasts (Saccharomyces cerevisiae) give most varieties of ale their characteristic fruity flavor and aroma. Lager brewing is a more recent invention, using yeasts (either a separate species, S. carlsbergensis, or a subspecies of S. cerevisiae) that prefer colder temperatures, from 39 to 54°. Unlike ale yeasts, lager yeasts remain suspended in the wort through fermentation, settling to the bottom when the sugar supply runs out, and are thus known as "bottom-fermenting."

CONDITIONING When the fermentation is complete or nearly so, the immature or "green" beer is typically transferred to another closed vessel to mature. For traditional British cask-conditioned or "real" ale, this takes place when the fermentation is not quite complete; most of the yeast is skimmed off the top, and the hazy, still active beer goes into the cask in which it will be delivered to the pub and from which it will be served. The fermentation continues in the cask, gently carbonating the beer as the flavor mellows and the beer becomes clear. The ale is ready to serve within just a few days, and once opened, it should be consumed within a couple of days. Bottled ales are conditioned in larger tanks, and also mature in a relatively short time.

For lagers, the conditioning is a much slower process, carried out at colder temperatures. Bottom-fermenting yeasts probably evolved in the cold-winter regions of central Europe, especially Bavaria and Bohemia. Until the invention of refrigeration, Bavarian brewers found that their beer tended to spoil in the summer, so they brewed large quantities in the spring and stored barrels of beer in caves, sometimes cooled with ice brought down from the Alps. As they tapped the barrels through the summer, they found that the long, cold storage (lager simply means to store) improved the flavor and clarity of the beer. Modern refrigeration allows for year-round production of lagers and a consistency of style. The classic European lagers are now lagered for around three months, while most large domestic brands are ready for bottling after about three weeks.

The distinction between lager and ale is sometimes blurred. Many North American ales are fermented warm (with either strain of yeast), then lagered at low temperature, a style sometimes called cream ale, American ale, or lager ale.* Düsseldorf altbier ("old-style," that is, top-fermenting) and most Bavarian wheat beers are also brewed with ale yeasts and then lagered cold; both are much maltier than most American ales. Steam beer, a style which arose in 19th-century San Francisco and is now a trademark of the Anchor Brewing Company, is another hybrid. Lager yeasts fermenting at ale temperatures in especially shallow containers produce a malty, flavorful beer with much of the fruitiness of an ale.

Whatever the method of conditioning, the beer may need a late boost in the fermentation process to provide the desired degree of carbonation. One way to achieve this is to add a fresh culture of yeast and a dose of sugar. Another method, known as kräusening, is to add some actively fermenting wort from anther batch of beer. Some breweries skip this step and introduce carbon dioxide into the beer under pressure, as in other carbonated beverages.

CLARIFICATION Except for a few specialty beers, most consumers expect crystal clarity in the glass, so most finished beers are filtered to remove any traces of dead yeast cells or other sediment. Some go through a preliminary "fining" step, in which an added ingredient such as clay, gelatin, or insinglass settles to the bottom, attracting proteins and other sediments with it. (Strips or chips of certain hardwoods also have some fining effect; "beechwood aging" is a matter of clarification, not flavor.)

PACKAGING After filtration, the beer is held under pressure until it is ready to be packaged into bottles, cans, or kegs. Most bottles and cans go right to a pasteurizing step, in which heat destroys any remaining yeasts or other spoilage organisms. Keg beer is usually not pasteurized, as it will be kept cold until it is served. Some bottled beers are not pasteurized, relying instead on a combination of very cold storage and micro-filtration to produce a sterile beer. After a short period to settle down after the packaging process, the beer is ready to drink (see Storing and Serving Beer, page 21).

A few beers, including German hefe-weizen wheat beers and some small brewery ales, are bottled right after kräusening, and undergo their final fermentation in the bottle, like Champagne. With time, the yeast will form a sediment in the bottle, which will remain behind if you pour the beer carefully. If you get a little in your glass, don't worry; it's perfectly safe to drink and even contains some extra vitamins, but it will give a yeasty flavor to the beer, and it has some laxative properties.

*Eckhardt, p. 56–7.

Index

Italic numbers indicate photographs.

adjuncts, 14
alcohol, in beer, 10, 27, 125
ale vs. beer, 10
ale, 12, 53, 99, 114, 125 (*see also* Brown Ale,
    Pale Ale, Porter, Stout)
    American, 15, 126
    amber, 10
    Belgian, 12, 16, 22
    blond, 15
    cream, 15
    Duck Braised in, 120, *121*
    English, 16
    Irish, 16
    Trappist, 16
almonds, 20
altbier, 16, 126
amber lager, 15, 50, 53, 96
American lager, 20, 50
Anchor Brewing Company, 126
    Steam Beer, 58
    Liberty Ale, 15
Anita's Nachos, 26
antipasto, 34
    Platter, *24,* 35, 60
Apple-Ginger Cake, Elaine's, 100
apples, 70
apricots, 117
Asian beer, 105
astringency, in beer, 17
Autumnal Italian Menu, 60

Bahia, 118
barbecue sauce, plum, 92
Barbecued Chicken, Jamaican, *98,* 99
Barbecued Ribs with Plum Sauce, 92
Barbecues, Picnics and 86
barley wine, 17, 125
basil, 72
Bass Ale, 15, 20, 120
Bavaria, 125
Bavarian Weizen, 17
beans, 75

Beck's, 14
beef, 89
    and Onions Braised in Beer, 114
    with beer, 15, 16, 19
beer
    aging, 14
    alcoholic content, 10, 27, 125
    and Food, 17
    and Other Good Foods, 8
    as Food, 39
    "belt," 12
    calories in, 10
    dark, 15, 118
    defined, 11
    dry, 17
    glasses, 22
    in restaurants, 12
    "lawnmower," 14
    light, 14
    matching with food, 107
    menu planning and, 23
    Mexican, 14, 15, 20, 48, 85
    nutritional values, 39
    prices, 10
    Purity Law, 11
    serving, 21
    Steam, 15, 126
    storing, 21
    strength of, 27
    styles of, 11, 12, *13,* 124
    super-premium, 15
    vs. ale, 10
    with spicy foods, 14
Beer Batter Fish & Chips, 66
Beer Biscuits, 54, 111
Beer-Steamed Clams, *46,* 50, 108
Beer: A Food-Friendly Beverage, 10
Beets, Paula's Marinated, 34, 35
Belgian ale, 12, 16, 22
Belgian cooking, 114
Berliner Weisse, 16, 125
Biscuits, Beer, 54
Bistec Criolla, *112,* 113
Bitter, 15
bitterness, in beer, 21
blond ale, 15

Bock, 10, 15, 108, 124, 125
Bohemia, 14, 125
Borrow, George, 41
bottom-fermenting, 14, 125
Braised Lamb Shanks with Olives, 60, 111
Braised Salmon with Cumin, 108, *109*
Braised Sausages and Polenta, *76,* 77
Brazilian Chicken Baked in Dark Beer, *102,* 118
breadsticks, 26
Brewing Process, The, 124
brewing, history of, 11
brewpubs, 7, 12
Brown Ale, 16, 100
Brussels, 11
Brussels lace, 23
Budweiser, 7, 14, 124
Burton-on-Trent, 11

Cake, Elaine's Apple-Ginger, 100
Calamari Fritti, 28, *29*
Calamari Vinaigrette Sandwich, 90
calories in beer, 10, 39
Campaign for Real Ale (CAMRA), 12
Canada, 15
carbonation, 126
Carbonnade Flamande, 114
Caribbean cooking, 99
Carlsberg, 14
Cashews, Ginger, 30
caul fat, 96
Celery Root Salad, 34, 35
Ceviche, 33, 80
Charcoal-Roasted Pork Loin, 58, 110
chard, red, 96
cheese, 74
    Board with Assorted Beers, 41
    Cornbread, 55
    for Dessert, 42
    sauce, with beer, 16
    with beer, 15, *18,* 19
Chesterton, G.K., 45
chicken, 58, 89
    Brazilian, Baked in Dark Beer, *102,* 118
    Jamaican Barbecued, *98,* 99
    Pot Pies, Ham and, 79
    roast, 115

chicken (cont.)
    smoked, 50
    Smoked, and Arugula Salad, 61
    with beer, 20
Child, Julia, 78, 82
chile(s), 19, 20, 23, 55
    chipotle, 48
    dried, 81
    habanero, 99
    Peanuts, Sichuan, 31
Chile-with-an-E, Rio Grande, 83
chili, 83
Chimay Ale, 16
Chinese cooking, 20, 39, 72, 90, 122
Chinese Five Flavors, 17
Chipotle Chiles, Shrimp Ball Soup with, 48, *49*
Chupe de Elote y Papas, *52, 53*
Chutney, Mango, 74
citrus, 19
clams, 31
    Beer-Steamed, 50
clarification, 126
cockles, 50
Cologne, 16
conditioning, 125
Cooking with Beer, 20
Coors, 7, 14
coppa, 35
coriander, 20
corn
    and Potato Stew, Peruvian, *52, 53*
    in beer, 14
    sweet, 58
cornbread, 31, 75
    Skillet, 55
Cornish hens, 119
    on the Grill, 99
Cost, Bruce, 43
couscous, 117
Couve, 118
crabmeat, 48
craft breweries, 12
cream ale, 15, 126
cumin, 20, 108
cured meats, with beer, 19
curry powder, 69

Curry, Vegetable Masala, *68,* 69
Czechoslovakia, 14

dark beer, 15, 118
dessert, 42
    with beer, 16
dextrins, 16, 17, 124
Dickens, Charles, 28
Dinner for Company, 102
Doppelbock, 12, 15, 42, 117, 125
Dos Equis, 15, 21, 57, 80
double Bock, see Doppelbock
dry beer, 17
Duck
    Braised in Ale, 120, *121*
    Breasts, Grilled, with Sichuan Pepper-
        corns, 58, 122
    cutting up, 120
    with beer, 19
Dunkel lager, 15
Düsseldorf, 16, 126
Duvel ale, 16

eggnog, 43
EKU Edelbock, 108
Elaine's Apple-Ginger Cake, 100
England, 66
ethnic foods, with beer, 19
European lagers, 126

fennel, 63
fermentation, 11, 125
festbier, 78
feta cheese, 36
Feta Salad, Lentil and, 35
Fettuccine with Smoked Fish and Sweet Corn,
    58, *59*
Filo Packets, Sweet Pepper, 36, *37*
filtering, 126
fining, 126
first courses, 46
Fish
    & Chips, Beer Batter, 66
    Filets, Kung Pao, 106
    Grilled, with Mustard Glaze, 97
    Pan-Fried, with Malaysian Bean Sauce,
        104, 105

sauce, 72
skewer test for, 97
smoked, 58
with beer, 16, 20
Five Flavors, Chinese, 17
Fleur de Lys, 113
Food, Beer and, 17
Frambozen, 17
Fresh Cornbread, 55
Fried Okra, 31, 54
Fried Squid, 28
frying tips, 67

Galinha com Cerveja, 118
garam masala, 69
Garlic Prawns Grilled in Foil, 58, 90, 91
garlic, 19, 20
    Browned, Shrimp with, *32,* 33
Garnet yams, 82
Germany, 15
ginger, 20, 100
    Cashews, 30
Ginger East to West, 43
Goldstein, Joyce, 40
Gösser Stiftsbräu, 60
Greece, 20
Green Chile Cornbread, 55
green peppercorns, 95
Grill, A Summer Menu from the, 58
Grilled Duck Breasts with Sichuan Pepper-
    corns, 58, 122
Grilled Fish with Mustard Glaze, 97
Grilled Shark with Assorted Salsas, 93
Grilled White Sausages with Red Chard, 96
Guinness Extra Stout, 16, 21
Gumbo, Smoked Turkey, 50

Ham
    and Cheese Sandwich, The Ultimate,
        89
    and Chicken Pot Pies, 79
    and Peas, Risotto with, *56, 57*
Hash, Two-Potato, 82, *83*
hefe-weizen, 126
Heileman's Special Export, 15
Heineken, 14

Henninger, 20
Henry Weinhard's Private Reserve, 15
Hogan, Paula, 88
Holiday Wassail Bowl, 43
home brewing, 12
hops, 11, 21, 124
　　and fat, 19
　　with spicy foods, 19

Imperial Stout, 16, 45, 100, 125
India Pale Ale, 15, 19, 95
Indian cooking, 20, 39
Indonesian food, with beer, 20
ingredients, 23
international-style lager, 14, 34, 95, 105, 122
Italian Menu, Autumnal, 60
Italy, 15, 19, 20, 34

Jackson, Michael, 79
Jamaican Barbecued Chicken, *98*, 99
Jerk Thighs, *98*, 99
jicama, 80
Johnson, Samuel, 74

keg beer, 126
Keller, Hubert, 113
kosher salt, 23
kräusening, 126
Kriek, 17
Kung Pao Fish Filets, 106

lactic acid, 16
lactose, 16
lager ale, 126
lager, 12, 14, 17, 53, 78, 80, 85, 96, 99, 113,
　　117, 125, 126
　　amber, 15, 50
　　dark, 15, 80, 119
　　dark German, 15, 20
　　Dunkel, 15, 20
　　Dutch, 14
　　export, 14
　　international-style, 14, 34, 95, 105, 122
　　Mexican, 14, 15, 20, 48, 85
　　Munich, 15, 20, 22, 78
　　northern German, 14

pale, 14, 50
　　standard American, 14, 20, 50
lagering, 14
Lamb
　　Satay with Peanut Sauce, 88
　　Shanks, Braised, with Olives, 60, 111
　　with beer, 15
Lambic, 17
"lawnmower beer," 14
Lentil and Feta Salad, 35
light beer, 14
"liquid bread," 11
Löwenbräu, 14, 20
Lunches and Simple Suppers, 64

Mackeson's Triple Stout, 16
Major Grey's chutney, 74
Malaysian Bean Sauce, Pan-Fried Fish with,
　　104, 105
Malaysian cooking, 88, 105
malt liquor, 17
malt, 11
　　Vienna, 15
malting, 124
Mango Chutney, 74
Märzen beer, 15, 77, 125 (*see also* Oktoberfest
　　beer)
mashing, 124
Matching Beer and Ethnic Cuisines, 19
meat, with beer, 16
Meatballs, Spice Route, 39
Mediterranean foods, 19
merguez, 40
Mexican beer, 14, 15, 20, 48, 85
Mexican cooking, 7, 20, 80
Mexican Salsa Cruda, 93
mezes, 20
microbreweries, 7, 12
Middle Eastern cooking, 19, 20, 39
Milk Stout, 45
Miller High Life, 14
mole poblano, 80, 81
Molson's Ale, 15
monasteries, brewing in, 11
Moretti "La Rossa," 15, 60
Moroccan cooking, 117

Munich, 11
Munich lager, 15, 20, 22, 78
mussels, 50
mustard glaze, 97

Nachos, Anita's, 26
nam pla, 72
Navy Beans and Cornbread, 75
Negra Modelo, 80
Neto, Valmor, 118
Newcastle Brown Ale, 16, 57
nibbles, 31
Nibbles, Snacks, and Party Food, 24
Noche Buena, 80
noodles, 72
North African cooking, 19, 20
nuoc mam, 72
nuts, seasoned, 30

oatmeal, in beer, 16
Oatmeal Stout, 45
oil, 23, 67
Okra, Fried, 31, 54
Oktoberfest beer, 42, 77 (*see also* Märzen
　　beer)
olive oil, 20
olives, 19, 35, 111
Olympia, 7
onions, 114
Optimator, 15
oregano, 19
oysters, 16, 31

packaging, 126
Pale Ale, 15, 42, 50, 61, 82, 96, 111, 120,
　　124
pale lager, 10, 14, 50
Pan-Fried Fish with Malaysian Bean Sauce,
　　104, 105
Papaya-Grapefruit Salsa, 93
party food, 24
Pasteur, Louis, 11
pasteurizing, 126
Pâté, Pistachio and Green Peppercorn, *94,* 95
Paula's Marinated Beets, 34, 35
Paulaner, 15

peanut oil, 67
Peanut Sauce, Lamb Satay with, 88
Peanuts, Sichuan Chile, 31
peas, 57
pepper, 20, 23
 Sweet, Filo Packets, 36, *37*
peppercorns
 green, 95
 Sichuan, 31, 122
peppers, sweet, 20
 roasted and peeled, 35, 61
Peruvian Corn and Potato Stew, *52,* 53
Picnics and Barbecues, 86
Pils, 14
Pilsener, *see* Pilsner
Pilsner, 14, 20, 33, 34, 50, 58, 60, 61, 82, 95, 99, 124
Pilsner Urquell, 14, 108
Pilzn, 11, 14
Pistachio and Green Peppercorn Pâté, *94,* 95
pizza, 20
Ploughman's Lunch, 74
plum sauce, 92
polenta, 77, 111, 120
pork, 89
 Chops, Smothered, with Apples, 70
 Loin, Charcoal-Roasted, 58, 110
 with beer, 19
Porter, 10, 16, 42, 45, 113
Portugal, 19
Pot Pies
 Ham and Chicken, 79
 Turkey Mole, 80
potatoes, 53, 82, 111
 sweet, 82
poultry, with beer, 16
Prawns, Garlic, Grilled in Foil, 58, 90, *91*
premium beer, 14
Pretzels, 26
price of beer, 10

Rabbit Couscous with Apricots, *116,* 117
red meat, beer with, 15
Red Tail Ale, 15
Reinheitsgebot, 11
Reuben Sandwich à la Dijonnaise, *64,* 71

Ribs, Barbecued with Plum Sauce, *86, 92*
rice
 for risotto, 57
 in beer, 14
 Pudding with Stout, *44,* 45
Rio Grande Chile-with-an-E, 83
Risotto with Ham and Peas, *56,* 57
Russian Stout, 16

salads
 Celery Root, 34, 35
 Lentil and Feta, 35
 Smoked Chicken and Arugula, 61
 Warm, with Sausage and Fennel, *62,* 63
salami, dry, 35
salmon
 beer with, 15
 Braised, with Cumin, 108, *109*
Salmonburgers, 90
salsa, 93
salt, 23
Salvator, 15
Samuel Adams' Boston Lager, 15
Samuel Smith's Pale Ale, 15
 Nut Brown Ale, 16
 Strong Stout, 16
sandwiches, 89, 90
 Reuben, à la Dijonnaise, 71
Satay, Lamb, with Peanut Sauce, 88
sauces
 peanut, 88
 plum, 92
 Spicy Tomato, 40
sauerkraut, 71
 Braised, Sausages with, 78
sausages, 31, 63
 beer with, 15, 19
 Braised, and Polenta, *76, 77*
 Grilled White, with Red Chard, 96
 types of, 78
 with Braised Sauerkraut, 78
scallops, 31
Scotch bonnet pepper, 99
Scotch woodcock, 70
seafood, 108
seasoned nuts, 30

serving beer, 21
 glasses, 22
 temperature, 26
Shakespeare, William, 111
Shark, Grilled, with Assorted Salsas, 93
shellfish, 20
 with beer, 16
shrimp, 53 (*see also* prawns)
 Ball Soup with Chipotle Chiles, 48, *49*
 with beer, 20
 with Browned Garlic, *32, 33*
Sichuan Chile Peanuts, 31
Sichuan peppercorns, 31, 122
Side Dishes and First Courses, 46
Sierra Nevada Pale Ale, 15
 Porter, 16
Singaporean cooking, 105
Singha beer, 20, 72
skewer test for fish, 97
Skillet Cornbread, 55
smoked chicken, 50
 and Arugula Salad, 61
Smoked Fish and Sweet Corn, Fettuccine with, 58, *59*
Smoked Turkey Gumbo, 50
Smothered Pork Chops with Apples, 70
snacks, 24
soft-shell clams, 50
Soup, Shrimp Ball, with Chipotle Chiles, 48, *49*
South American cooking, 113
Southeast Asian cooking, 20, 72, 88
southern European foods, 19
Spaghetti alla Puttanesca, *8,* 60
Spain, 19, 33
spareribs, with beer, 20
Spaten, 15
 Franziskaner Hefe-Weissbier, 58
Spice Route Meatballs, 39
spices, 19, 20
spicy foods, beer with, 14, 15
Spicy Tomato Sauce, 40
Spring Seafood Menu, 108
Square One restaurant, 40
squid, 53
 cleaning, 28

130

Fried, 28
    Stir-Fried, and Noodles with Basil, 72, 73
St. Pauli Girl, 14, 60
standard American lager, 14, 20, 50
Steak with Diced Vegetable Relish, *112*, 113
Steam Beer, 15, 126
Stew, Peruvian Corn and Potato, *52*, 53
Stir-Fried Squid and Noodles with Basil, 72, 73
storing beer, 21
Stout Porter, 16
Stout, 10, 12, 16, 42, 45, 99, 100, 114, 124
    Imperial, 16
    Rice Pudding with, *44, 45*
    Russian, 16
strong ale, 17, 125
styles of beer, 11, 12
sugars, unfermentable, 16, 17, 124
summer menu, 58
super-premium beer, 7, 15
suppers, simple, 64
sweet corn, 58
Sweet Pepper Filo Packets, 36, *37*
sweetness, in beer, 21

tapas, 19, 33
terrine, 95
texture of foods, in matching beer, 19
Thai cooking, 20, 72
Thai Tomato Salsa, 93
thyme, 19
Tomato Sauce, Spicy, 40
top-fermenting, 14, 125
Trappist ale, 16, 114
tropical cuisines, with beer, 19
Tsingtao, 122
Tuborg, 14
turkey, 58, 89
    Gumbo, Smoked, 50
    Mole Pot Pies, 80
    Sandwich, 89
Two-Potato Hash, 82, *83*

unfermentable sugars, 16, 17, 124

Vegetable Masala Curry, *68, 69*
Vienna malt, 15
Warm Salad with Sausage and Fennel, *62, 63*
Wassail Bowl, Holiday, 43
Weissbier, 16, 22

Weizenbier, 16
Welsh Rabbit, 70
wheat beer, 10, 12, 16, 17, 126
white beer, 16
winter warmer, 17
Wolfert, Paula, 117

Xingu, 119

yeast, 11, 14, 17, 125, 126
Young's ale, 15
Yugoslavia, 19

zucchini, 54

131